BeaD
Bugs

Cute, Creepy, and Quirky Projects to Make
with Beads, Wire, and Fun Found Objects

AMY KOPPERUDE

Copyright © 2013 Creative Publishing international, Inc.

All rights reserved. No part of this work covered by the copyrights hereon may be reproduced or used in any form or by any means—graphic, electronic, or mechanical, including photocopying, recording, taping of information on storage and retrieval systems—without the written permission of the publisher.

First published in the United States of America by Creative Publishing international, Inc., a member of Quayside Publishing Group
400 First Avenue North
Suite 300
Minneapolis, MN 55401
1-800-328-3895
www.creativepub.com

ISBN: 978-1-58923-732-2

10 9 8 7 6 5 4 3 2 1

Library of Congress Cataloging-in-Publication Data available

Copy Editor: Ellen Goldstein
Proofreader: Karen Ruth
Book Design: Sporto
Cover Design: Sporto
Page Layout: Sporto
Interior Photographs: Amy Kopperude

Printed in China

To my daughters Greta and Josephine
who always inspire me to be everything that I am

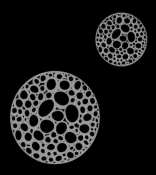

contents

introduction

Your backyard is teeming with life. From slimy and slithery to colorful and shimmery, the bugs and small creatures that move about under rocks, through underground tunnels, and beneath the water's surface, even those that scamper in the trees or float on the breeze, are nature's wonders.

And they come to life in this book in a way that might never have occurred to you. *Bead Bugs* provides 23 different projects to help you experiment with a type of beading that includes found and recycled objects.

Tired of making the same necklaces and earrings? This book presents beaded projects that are more than fashion accessories or jewelry pieces. When you shop for craft materials, think about how you can recreate the world around you with beads and other findings.

After paging through *Bead Bugs*, you may want to visit your local bead store and think about how different shapes and colors of beads can be used to create altered versions of these small living beings. Then, step out of the bead aisle, or even the bead store, and explore other materials that can be used to embellish your creation: ribbon, spacer bars, yarn and fabric, nuts and washers from the hardware store, metal screen, twigs and seeds from outside, even materials from the recycling bin. In a market flooded with both handmade and commercially made beading supplies, the world is your oyster. (Heck, you can probably make an oyster using beads and other materials.) Take apart something broken to see if you can imagine something new. Whether you rely on step-by-step instructions or would rather think outside of the box to create, you will find that many of the creature creations in this book have similar constructions and you need only to vary technique and beads to come up with your own bug once you have mastered some of the bugs presented here.

Any one of these beaded projects affords an opportunity for a handmade gift, the very best kind of gift there is. Soon, it won't just be your backyard teeming with life.

tools & materials

Only a few tools are needed to make the projects in this book. You may already have what you need, especially if you have dabbled in making bead jewelry. All of these tools and materials can be found at your craft store.

TOOLS

Round-Nose Pliers (a): Use round-nose pliers to create loops when beginning a spiral or finishing ends.

Flat-Nose Pliers (b): Use flat-nose pliers to make flat spirals (as for antennae), secure wire loop closures, bend wire at a specific angle, and tighten or adjust pieces of wire.

Wire Cutters (c): Use wire cutters to cut wire to the desired length or trim wire for finishing touches.

Mini Butane Torch (d): Use a butane torch for flame-coloring copper screen for bug wings.

Rotary Tool (e): Use the rotary tool and small drill bits for drilling holes as necessary for certain beaded bugs (e.g., Hermit Crab Cage Companion, page 48 and Caged Owl Tree Topper, page 110).

WIRE AND CORD

18- or 12-Gauge (f): Heavier gauge wires are typically only suitable for very large beads or structures (e.g., bat mobile, page 76); 12-gauge wire is found in the floral section of most craft stores.

20-Gauge: This heavy-gauge wire works well for hangers (e.g., Seahorse Ornament, page 36) and other strong supports (e.g., Mosquito Candle Clinger, page 30).

22-Gauge: This gauge of wire is the preferred thickness for projects that require more stability (e.g., Spider Pin, page 18). It's just pliable enough to be considered sturdy but not so thick that most seed and bugle beads won't slide onto the wire, as happens with the 20-gauge wire.

24-Gauge: Somewhat more pliable than 22-gauge wire, 24-gauge wire works well for threading beads that are too small to fit on 22-gauge wire.

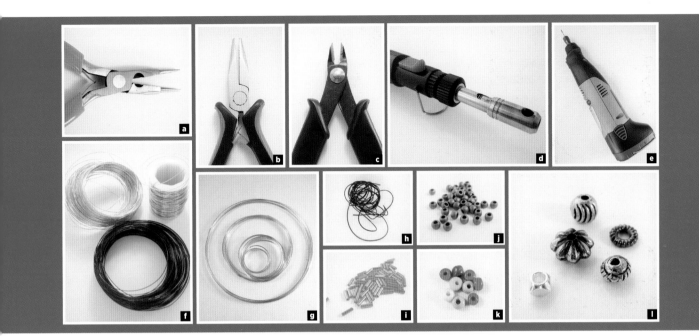

26- or 28-Gauge: Floral wire is a common 28-gauge wire, which can be used for projects that are light-weight (e.g., Spider Suncatcher, page 22) or for projects that require sliding beads onto two pieces of wire (e.g., Dragonfly Wine Glass Charms, page 12, Ladybug Hair Spirals, page 26, Fireflies in a Jar, page 54). It is also very easy to maneuver with hands rather than tools.

Memory Wire (g): Memory wire is preshaped circular wire that is used for making hoop-shaped necklaces, spiral bracelets, and rings.

Jelly Cord (h): A lightweight, stretchy cord used for beaded bracelets that is effective for hanging the Spider Suncatcher (page 22) and attaching the slug to the hair comb (page 106).

BEADS

Bugle Beads (i): Small tubelike beads typically made of glass

Seed Beads (j): Very small round beads used for intricate designs

E Beads (k): E beads or beads with a ⅗ measurement are slightly larger than seed beads and are often solid colored plastic or glass and simple in design

Spacer Beads (l): The beads used to separate or give space to the surrounding beads; they are typically smaller or shorter than other beads and often are metal

(continued)

Rondelle/Disk Beads (a): Flat saucerlike beads that have a shorter height than width

Bicone Beads (b): Small faceted beads that are decorative and work well as spacers for bead bugs

Drop/Teardrop Beads (c): Pear-shaped beads with a hole that runs through the narrow tip or through the center of the bead from narrow end to widest end

Glow Beads (d): Phosphorescent beads that glow after being exposed to light for a short time

Focal Beads (e): Beads that are typically larger than the others but vary in terms of shape or design to make a project more aesthetically pleasing and proportional

Crimp Beads (f): Short metal tubelike beads that are pinched closed to keep other beads in place or to finish ends of bracelets and necklaces

Hooked Crimp Beads (g): Small metal findings with a cap for threading wire and two flat sides that pinch together around fiber or wire

Spacer Bars (h): Barlike beads with several holes for threading wide bracelets or watches

Bead Caps (i): Cone-shaped beads used to accentuate the tips or ends of other beads, especially focal beads (Seahorse Ornament, page 36, and Firefly wings, page 59)

OTHER MATERIALS

Flat Glass Marbles (j): Typically used inside vases, these marbles can be made into small charms and used for the Spider Suncatcher, page 22

Eye Pin (k): A long pin/wire with a looped finished end for securing beads (e.g., Bug-Eye Fishing Jig, page 60)

Head Pin (l): A long pin/wire with a flat finished end for securing beads (e.g., Caged Owl Tree Topper, page 110)

Jump Ring (m): A round metal ring used to link head pins or other metal loops in jewelry making (e.g., owl cage drop beads, pages 112–113)

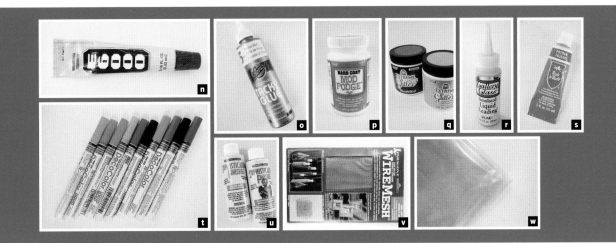

E-6000 Craft Adhesive (n): A reliable adhesive used for beaded crafts

Craft Glue (o): An adhesive that works on surfaces such as paper and wood (e.g., picture frame sand garden, pages 46–47)

Acrylic Sealer (p): A gluelike protective coat that dries clear and is often used for decoupage (e.g., Stick Insect focal bead, page 96)

Glitter-Infused Clear Coat (q): A gluelike coat that dries clear and lends shimmer to a project (e.g., bat wings, pages 78–79)

Simulated Liquid Leading (r): Simulated liquid leading is used to create imitation stained glass

Wax-Based Faux Patina (s): A patina that can be rubbed on wood or metal surfaces, then buffed to lend an aged look to an object (e.g., fly wings, pages 72–73)

Opaque Paint Markers (t): Useful for drawing on glass

Antique Finish Metallic Paint (u): Metallic paint that gives metal an aged look

Copper Mesh (v): An 80-mesh woven copper screen that can be cut, bent, and burnished for wings (dragonfly wings, pages 16–17)

Clear Heavy Vinyl (w): Used for delicate bug wings because it keeps its shape (mosquito wings, pages 34–35)

dragonfly
wine glass charms

*W*ine glass charms add some extra pizzazz to your party and help your guests identify which drink belongs to them. Make these charms for a hostess or housewarming gift.

MATERIALS

SUPPLIES

» One 9" (23 cm) piece of 26-gauge wire

» One seed or E bead for the tail

» Various tube and round beads measuring 2" to 2 ½" (5 to 6.4 cm) in length when threaded together

» Two seed beads for the eyes

» 2" x 3" (5 to 7.6 cm) piece of 80-mesh woven copper (*see* Resources, page 128)

» E-6000 craft adhesive

TOOLS

» Wire cutters

» Flat-nose pliers

» Round-nose pliers

» Fine-point permanent marker

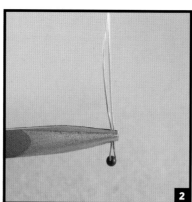

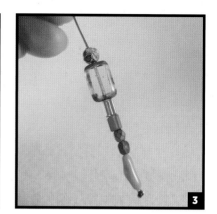

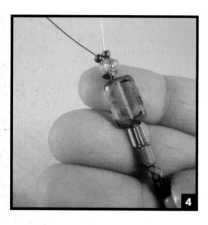

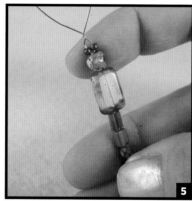

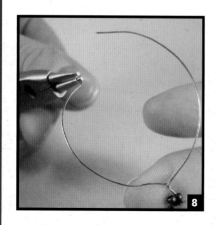

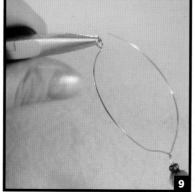

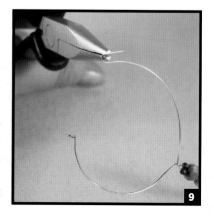

Thorax & Abdomen

1. Use wire cutters to cut a piece of 26-gauge wire approximately 9" (23 cm) in length. Thread the seed or E bead onto the center of the wire, and fold the wire in half.

2. Pinch the wires together just above the bead. Use flat-nose pliers if preferred.

3. Thread the tube and/or round beads onto both pieces of wire that are now pinched together. When approximately 2" to 2 ½" (5 to 6.4 cm) of beads have been threaded onto the wires, finish with a round bead to make the dragonfly head.

4. Slightly pull apart the two pieces of wire, and thread a seed bead onto each wire.

5. Holding the two seed beads evenly in place for the dragonfly eyes, twist the two pieces of wire together twice and as close to the eyes as possible to secure them.

6. Use your fingertips to smooth the ends of the wire into a circular shape so that they meet together to form a hoop.

7. Trim the excess wire so that the hoop is approximately 1 ½" (3.8 cm) in diameter.

8. Make a loop at one end of the wire with round-nose pliers.

9. With flat-nose pliers, bend the loop so that it is straight up and down. Bend over the other end of the wire to form a hook.

10. Slip the hook through the loop; this is how the wine glass charm can be connected and disconnected around a wine glass stem or bottle neck.

Wings

11. Fold the piece of copper mesh in half, short end to short end.

12. Use a fine-point permanent marker to draw one side of the wings (two wings) of the dragonfly on the copper mesh so that the wing centers face the center fold.

TRY THiS:

Instead of finishing the dragonfly with a hoop for a wine glass charm, attach a pin instead, or string numerous dragonflies across a ribbon as a garland.

Use a drop bead for the end of the tail and then use fewer beads for the rest of the body so that the whole length of the dragonfly's body is about 2" or 2½" (5 to 6.5 cm) long.

13. Starting at the fold, cut out the wings.

14. Open the wings and lay them flat. Then, slightly overlap the top wings over the bottom wings at the center, forming an accordian-like crease.

15. Gripping the copper wings with the flat-nose pliers, hold a mini butane torch approximately 1" (2.5 cm) from the wings to add color. Allow the flame to touch the wings for just a moment at a time until rainbow colors appears. If the flame touches the copper for too long, the rainbow effect turns to a burnished brown.

16. Add a dot of E-6000 craft adhesive to the bead below the dragonfly's head.

17. Press the wings onto the glued area, and allow to dry.

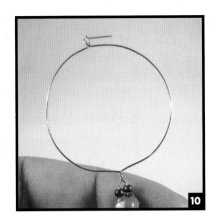

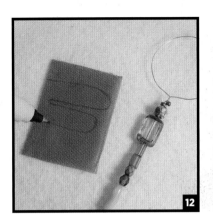

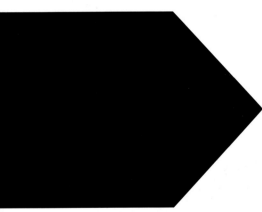

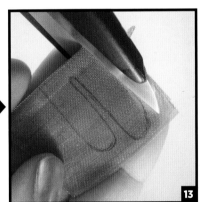

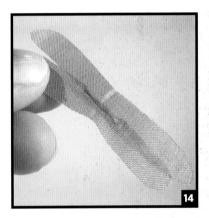

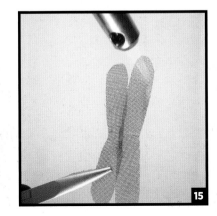

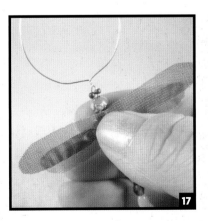

spider pin

Spiders are both feared and revered. This creepy crawly pin is no ordinary project, so consider the double takes you'll get if you pin it to your shoulder. Follow the variation for a suncatcher or add to Halloween decorations.

MATERIALS

SUPPLIES

» Two seed beads for the eyes
» Two focal beads, one about half or three-quarters the size of the other (head/thorax and abdomen of the spider)
» One spacer bead (rondelle bead or similar size/shape)
» Five 6" (15 cm) pieces of 22- or 24-gauge wire
» Forty-eight #3 bugle beads
» Thirty-two seed beads for the legs
» Sixteen E (⅝) beads or 4- to 5-mm beads
» E-6000 craft adhesive

TOOLS

» Wire cutters
» Round-nose pliers

Abdomen, Thorax, & Head

1. Using the wire cutters, cut five pieces of wire approximately 6" (15 cm) in length. One of the wires is used to thread the body and eyes of the spider. The other four wires are used for the spider legs.

2. Thread two seed beads onto one of the pieces of wire. Move the beads to the center of the wire, and fold the wire in half. Pinch the two pieces of wire just beneath the beads while keeping the beads aligned for the eyes.

3. Thread the three beads chosen for the spider's body (focal bead, spacer bead, focal bead) onto the wire with the eyes in order of eyes, head, thorax, and abdomen. The spacer bead will help evenly space the spider's legs so they're easier to adjust at the center of the spider's body once all of the legs are beaded.

4. Use the wire cutters to shorten the remainder of the two wire pieces, leaving about ¼" (6 mm) of wire. Then, use the round-nose pliers to curve the wires into a tight loop. This not only keeps the body beads from sliding off but also keeps the legs from rotating around the spider body while they're being beaded.

5. Taking two wires at a time, wrap the wires first around the top of the center spacer bead at the center of the wires, crisscrossing the wire lengths underneath the spider and bringing them up to the front. Do the same with two more wires around the bottom of the center bead. Use flat-nose pliers to pull on the wires and ensure a snug fit around the center of the spider.

Legs

6. Once all of the leg wires are wrapped around the spider body, spread them out.

7. Be creative with the beading. You don't necessarily have to follow this order. Start with two #3 bugle beads, one seed bead, one E

bead or 4-/5-mm bead, one seed bead. Repeat this order one more time; finish with the bugle beads.

8. When finishing beading a leg, trim the excess wire with the wire cutters. Leave just enough wire (about ¼" [6 mm]) to create a loop with the round-nose pliers. If the wire is thin enough and the bead hole big enough, thread the end of the wire back into the bead.

9. Slightly bend each leg where the E or 4-/5-mm bead is located to give the spider its creepy angular legs.

10. Finish beading the other seven spider legs according to the instructions in Step 7. Take the time to make a few more minor adjustments to the legs so that they're angled as desired, and if the spider is a little loose (legs that spin around or a body frame that shifts too much), turn the spider upside-down, apply some E-6000 craft adhesive to places where the wires twist around the center body bead, and let the spider dry for a few hours before adhering the pin back.

Finishing Touches

11. When the spider is dry and sturdy, place the pin back on the underside of the spider where you want it, apply a small line of E-6000 craft adhesive, and place the pin.

TRY THiS:

Replace the focal bead with a found object like a watch or locket. To create fancier leg ends for the spider, make the loop into a spiral in Step 8.

spider suncatcher

I nvite some sparkle to any room by hanging this shiny spectacle in the window. The spider suncatcher is unlike run-of-the-mill rainbows, kites, and cloud suncatchers that typically brighten a space, and it's far more dimensional and colorful.

MATERIALS

SUPPLIES

» Two flat glass marbles
» Simulated liquid leading
» Opaque paint markers in varying colors
» Four 6" (15 cm) pieces of 22- or 24-gauge wire
» Wax or freezer paper
» Jelly cord
» Suction cup hook

TOOLS

» Small scissors
» Wire cutters
» Round-nose pliers

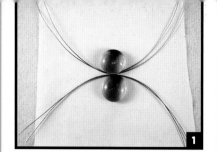

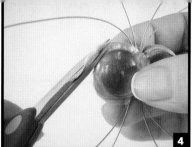

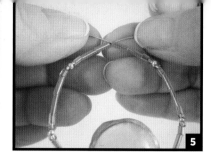

Abdomen & Thorax

1. Place two flat marbles next to one another on a small square of wax or freezer paper (smoother side up). Then center all four wires between the two marbles so that there is between ⅛" and ¼" (3 and 6 mm) of space between the marbles.

2. Squeeze a figure 8 of the simulated liquid leading around both marbles, being sure to fill up the space between the two marbles and coating the wires well. Apply enough liquid leading (⅛" [3 mm]) so that when it dries, all of the pieces will hold together (see tip below).

3. After a day or two, when the liquid leading dries firmly, carefully peel the spider body away from the wax or freezer paper. Double-check that the liquid leading on the underside of the spider is also dry. If not dry or if there are gaps where the liquid leading didn't quite fill in, touch up those areas with more liquid leading and allow to dry completely.

4. Using a small pair of scissors, trim the excess dried liquid leading from the spider to create clean lines around the spider.

Legs

5. Follow Steps 8 and 9 of the Spider Pin (page 21) to bead the legs of the spider suncatcher, but do not trim the excess wire from the top/front two legs. Instead, cross the wires at the ends.

TIP:

Slightly arch the wires in the positions you want them to be for beading so that they'll require less adjusting after the liquid leading (see Step 2) has dried.

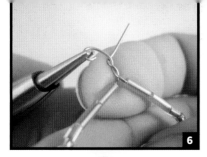

6. Twist the two pieces of wire twice. Now, trim the excess wires evenly with a pair of wire cutters, leaving about $\frac{5}{16}$" (8 mm) of wire. Use the round-nose pliers to bend the wires into two flat spirals.

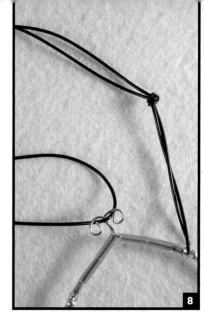

TRY THiS:

Paint the front and back of the glass marbles with glitter-infused clear coat (hologram) or another glitter glue that dries clear for added glitz.

Finishing Touches

7. Choose paint marker colors that match the colors of the beads on the spider's legs, and draw varying sizes of dots on the glass marbles.

8. Adjust the legs as desired, but consider keeping the legs flat so that the entire body is flat when hanging in a window. Cut a piece of jelly cord 6" to 9" (15 to 23 cm) in length. Fold it in half and tie the two ends into a square knot. Slip the folded end of the cord between the spaces of the flat spirals to hang the suncatcher on a suction cup hook in a bright, sunny window.

ladybug
hair spirals

This quick and easy project can be done in no time to add summer sparkle to your hair. These small, quaint ladybugs will fix up any 'do.

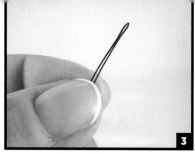

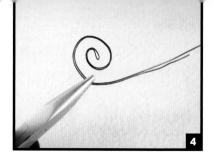

DIRECTIONS

1. Apply a thin layer of E-6000 craft adhesive to the area of one side of the red bead.

2. Use tweezers to gently and evenly place the four rhinestones to either side of the bead hole. Allow to dry.

Hair Spiral

3. Use the wire cutters to cut an 8" (20 cm) piece of black wire and fold it in half, pinching the folded end closed with flat-nose pliers.

TRY THiS:

Look for flat oval orange and yellow beads for more kinds of ladybugs.

4. Use the flat-nose pliers to form the folded piece of wire into a flat spiral, making two rounds, starting at the folded end. Allow approximately 2 ¼" (6 cm) of wire after making the spiral. If there is not enough wire, tighten the spiral.

5. Use the flat-nose pliers to make a 90-degree bend in the wire at the end of the spiral.

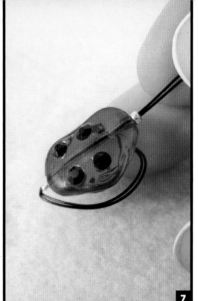

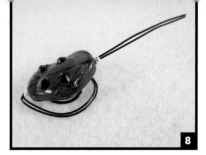

6. Slide one crimp bead onto the two wires all the way to the bend, and use the flat-nose pliers to pinch it firmly in place.

7. Slide the ladybug bead onto the two pieces of wire all the way to the crimp bead. Slide the other crimp bead onto the two pieces of wire. Be sure that the ladybug bead and the second crimp bead are tight against each other before using the flat-nose pliers to pinch the second crimp bead in place. The rhinestones may weigh down the top of the bead, causing it to flip over, but as the hair spiral is put in place, the ladybug can be adjusted correctly.

Adjust the coiled hair spiral as needed to shape the ladybug hair spiral into a workable piece of hair art.

Antennae

8. Trim the excess wire to approximately 1½" (4 cm).

9. Use the round-nose pliers to form each of the ladybug antennae into flat spirals.

mosquito
candle clinger

With mosquitoes the size of birds in some regions, this larger-than-life version can hover above a dashboard, hang suspended from a window, or, in this case, cling to a citronella votive holder to lend more atmosphere to a patio party.

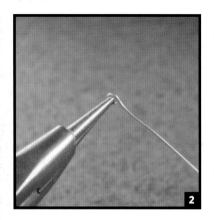

1. Use the wire cutters to cut the lengths of wire needed for this project. The 13" (33 cm) piece of wire will tether the mosquito to the rim of a citronella patio candle. The three pieces of 7" (18 cm) and 8" (20 cm) wire will be used for the

4. At the tip of the curved tube bead, use the round-nose pliers to make another loop, as small as possible, to finish off the proboscis.

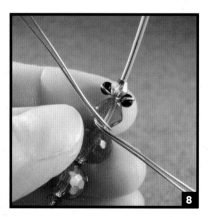

mosquito legs. The 4" (10 cm) piece of wire will be used to thread the body and proboscis of the mosquito. One of the 2" (5 cm) pieces of wire will be used for the eyes; the other will be used to attach the wings.

Abdomen, Thorax, Head & Proboscis

2. Starting with the 4" (10 cm) piece of wire, use the round-nose pliers to create a small closed loop at one end.

3. Thread the following beads in the following order: 6-mm bugle, bicone, 6-mm bugle, bicone, 6-mm bugle, bicone, 12-mm round, flat spacer, 12-mm round, diamond, bicone, curved tube. Use the wire cutters to remove excess wire to approximately 3/16" (5 mm).

Eyes

5. Continuing with a 2" (5 cm) piece of wire, wrap the wire from underneath (it doesn't matter which portion of the body is considered "underneath" at this point,

but the flat part of the diamond bead will be the top or bottom of the mosquito once the legs are put in place) and between the diamond and bicone bead, crisscrossing the wires over the top. Use the flat-nose pliers to pull the wire snugly between the two beads.

6. Thread one black seed bead on each end of the crisscrossed wire one at a time.

7. Trim the excess wire to within 1/4" (6 mm) of remaining wire, and use the round-nose pliers to curve the end of the wire underneath the mosquito's head for its eyes.

Legs

8. Wrap two of the 7" (18 cm) wires between the diamond and 12-mm beads starting at the top, and crisscross the wire lengths underneath the mosquito. Bring the

wires back up above the mosquito's body, pulling them snugly with the flat-nose pliers. Do the same with the 8" (20 cm) piece of wire between the foremost 12-mm bead and the spacer bead.

9. Spread out the wires so that the two foremost legs face forward and the other four legs face backward. For each of the foremost legs, begin beading in the following order with the following beads: 6-mm bugle, 9-mm bugle, round metal spacer, 9-mm bugle, 6-mm bugle, round metal spacer, 6-mm bugle, 9-mm bugle, 6-mm bugle, and 9-mm bugle. Finish each leg by creating a loop with the round-nose pliers.

10. For each of the four back legs, begin beading in the following order with the following beads: 6-mm bugle, 9-mm bugle, round metal spacer, 9-mm bugle, 6-mm bugle, round metal spacer, 6-mm bugle, 9-mm bugle, 6-mm bugle, 9-mm bugle, 6-mm bugle, 9-mm bugle.

12. Cut through both layers of vinyl around the wing so that both wings are the same shape and size.

13. Use the needle to punch through both layers of vinyl at the narrowest point of each wing.

14. Bend the 2" (5 cm) piece of wire into a horseshoe shape and thread both wings onto the wire so that the wings are centered on wire.

15. Wrap the wire underneath the body of the mosquito, and twist it tightly to secure the wings in place.

16. Trim the excess wire with the wire cutters, and use the round-nose pliers to curve and tuck the wire out of the way.

Hook Attachment

17. Leaving 1" (2.5 cm) of allowance at one end of the 13" (33 cm) piece of wire, wrap the end of the wire around and between the two 12-mm beads, crisscrossing the wire ends underneath, and twisting the short end (1" [2.5 cm] end) of the wire around the other 12" (30.5 cm) of wire close to the body of the mosquito. Use the flat-nose pliers to pinch the short end of the wire close to the long wire to keep the wire from scratching anyone or anything.

18. At the other end of the 13" (33 cm) piece of wire, fold 1" (2.5 cm) to create a hook. Hold the hook against the rim of the candle and wrap the wire around the rim and back to the hook. Slide the wire inside the hook.

Wings

11. Fold the piece of vinyl in half. Holding the folded end down, trace a long, thin oval wing ¾" (2 cm) wide by the length of the mosquito's body. Narrow the wing at one end.

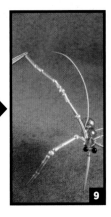

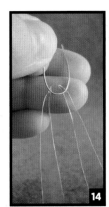

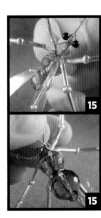

19. Then, bend the wire at a 90-degree angle and shape the rest of the wire—with the mosquito attached to the end—so that the mosquito hovers above and away from the candle flame.

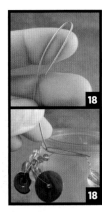

sea horse
ornament

This sea horse ornament may seem elaborate, but the trick to creating one successfully is in the choice of a wide array of bead styles.

MATERIALS

SUPPLIES

» One 24" (61 cm) piece of 28-gauge wire
» One 9" (23 cm) piece of 20-gauge wire
» Four 6-mm oval beads
» Three spacer beads
» One 8-mm round bead
» One large drop bead (approximately 28 mm) or oval bead for focal body piece of sea horse
» Approximately four 8-mm flat drop beads with side holes
» Approximatey three 3-mm rondelle or disk-shaped beads
» One 10-mm round flat bead
» One bendable bead cap proportional to flat round bead

» Three seed beads for snout of sea horse
» One 4-mm round bead for ear of sea horse
» Many seed beads for neck of sea horse
» One small cone-shaped bead cap or spacer bead for snout of sea horse
» One fin-shaped bead
» One 3-mm rhinestone
» E-6000 craft adhesive

TOOLS

» Wire cutters
» Round-nose pliers
» Flat-nose pliers
» Tweezers

1. Fold one third of the piece of wire in half, leaving one half of the folded wire an extra third longer than the other half. Slide one seed bead onto one half of the wire up to where the wire is folded. Use the round-nose pliers to pinch the wire

4. Continue sliding beads onto the shorter wire in the following order: 10-mm round flat bead, slightly bent bead cap, two seed beads, cone-shaped bead from the narrowest end, one seed bead.

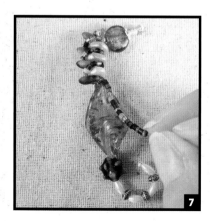

DIRECTIONS

together above the seed bead. This is the tip of the sea horse's tail.

2. Alternate sliding 4-mm oval beads and spacer beads onto both wires until the sea horse tail is 1½" (4 cm) long. Slide the round 8-mm bead and the large drop bead onto both wires.

3. Alternate sliding the four 8-mm drop beads and the three 3-mm disk-shaped beads onto both wires. Slightly bend into a curve. Spread the two wires apart so that the longest part of the wire is up out of the way.

Using the wire cutters, trim the excess wire to approximately ³⁄₁₆" (5 mm). Using the needle-nose pliers, create a small loop at the tip of the sea horse's snout.

5. Thread one 4-mm round bead for the sea horse's ear onto the remaining long wire. Fold the wire down in front of the sea horse, bring it to the back of the sea horse, and begin threading the seed beads onto the wire.

6. Continue threading seed beads onto the wire while wrapping the wire around and between the disk beads and small flat drop beads. At the base of the disk and small flat drop beads, pull the wire straight.

7. Thread seed beads onto the wire to measure the length of the large focal bead and lay the wire flat against the back of the bead (the back of the sea horse).

8. Loop the wire once around and between the large focal bead and the 8-mm round bead so that the remaining wire can be threaded with the sea horse fin.

9. Thread the fin-shaped bead onto the wire.

10. Loop the wire again around and between the large focal bead and the 8-mm round bead, pulling it taut.

11. Begin at the base of the fin-shaped bead and wrap the excess wire tightly around the fin-shaped bead to create a wire-wrapped base for the fin to give the bead more stability. Continue wrapping until the wrapped wire reaches the hole of the bead.

12. Push the excess wire through the hole, pull it taut with the flat-nose pliers, and trim it back with wire cutters.

13. Place a small dot of E-6000 craft adhesive on the round flat bead of the sea horse's head. Use a pair of tweezers to gently place the rhinestone on the dot of glue for the eye.

Directions for Ornament Hanger

14. Fold the 9" (23 cm) piece of 20-gauge wire into a V to create the center of the ornament hanger.

15. Thread the 9" (23 cm) piece of 20-gauge wire through the seed-beaded wire at the back of the sea horse's head up to the bend in the V.

16. Twist the ends of the wire two or three times, leaving approximately ½" to 1" (1.3 to 2.5 cm) of excess wire. Trim the excess wire to equal lengths.

17. Use the needle-nose pliers to form a flat spiral at each end of the excess wire at the top of the ornament hanger.

11

12

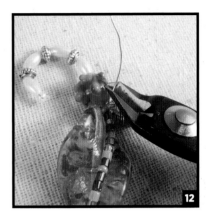

12

13

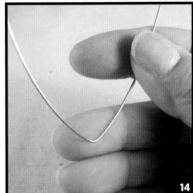

14

15

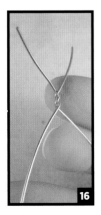

16

17

TRY THiS:

Instead of using a fin-shaped bead, make your own fin with baking clay (following the manufacturer's instructions). Insert a piece of wire through the fin while it's baking to ensure the fin has a bead hole so it will attach to the rest of the sea horse. Note: Steps 11 and 12 are unnecessary if making a fin with baking clay.

scorpion
sand garden

*T*he formidable scorpion, in beaded form, is far less intimidating in its new habitat on your desk or shelf, or in a Zen garden where you can arrange it in a bed of sand among a couple of smooth stones and drift away to your mental sanctuary.

MATERIALS

SUPPLIES

» One 18" (46 cm) piece of 24- or 20-gauge wire
» One 6" (15 cm) piece of 24-gauge wire
» Two 2" (5 cm) pieces of 24-gauge wire
» Approximately 12 varying size spacer bars
» Two round spacer beads for eyes
» Four round spacer beads for pincer arms
» One rectangular spacer bead for between eyes
» Four rectangular spacer beads (or similar) for pincer arms
» Three round spacer beads for tail
» Thirty-two bugle beads

» Thirteen 8-mm oval beads for legs, pincer arms, and tail
» Three porcupine quills (see Resources)
» Three 15-mm flat diamond-shape beads
» Thirty-three seed beads
» Small picture frame
» Sand
» Smooth stones
» E-6000 craft adhesive
» Craft glue

TOOLS

» Wire cutters
» Round-nose pliers
» Flat-nose pliers

1. Use the wire cutters to cut the lengths of wire needed for this project. The 18" (46 cm) piece of wire will be used for the body of the scorpion from the tail to the front pincers. A heavier gauge wire, such as 20-gauge, is preferable for the body of the scorpion unless the beads for the tail and pincer arms are too small to slide onto folded wire. The 24-gauge may be

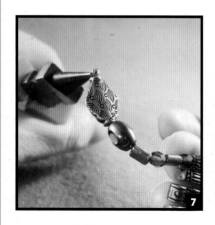

easier to work with. The four 6" (15 cm) pieces of wire will be used for the eight legs. The 2" (5 cm) pieces of wire are to secure spacer bars to the top of the scorpion after the legs have been beaded to hide exposed wire.

Tail

2. Fold the 18" (46 cm) piece of wire in half, and slide a seed bead to the center of the fold. Pinch the two wires closed under the seed bead with flat-nose pliers. Make sure the wire is pinched tightly.

3. Thread the beads for the tail in the following order: diamond-shaped bead, oval bead, spacer bead, oval bead, spacer bead, oval bead, spacer bead. The tail should measure close to 2" (5 cm) in length, so adjust the number of beads used based on that measurement. After the last spacer bead, separate the wires.

Abdomen & Thorax

4. Thread each wire through a short spacer bar so that the spacer bar is centered with the tail beads.

5. Continue threading the other spacer bars, giving the scorpion its plated, segmented look. Begin and finish the body of the scorpion with the smallest spacer bars. The body of the scorpion should measure approximately 2" (5 cm) long.

6. After threading the spacer bars, thread each wire end through the three beads used for the eyes and between the eyes so that a wire comes out each end for beading the pincers.

Pincers

7. Thread beads on each pincer arm in this order: round spacer, rectangle spacer bead, round spacer bead, rectangle spacer, oval bead, diamond-shape bead. With wire cutters, trim excess wire from the end of each pincer arm, leaving approximately ³⁄₁₆" (5 mm). With needle-nose pliers, form a small loop at the end of each arm.

8. Using the 6" (15 cm) wires for the legs, wrap two at a time between the first and second spacer bars at the head starting at the top of the scorpion and crisscrossing underneath. Bring the wires back to the top, and use the flat-nose pliers to pull the wires snugly between the spacer bars. Do the same with two more wires between the second and third spacer bars.

9. Thread the beads on each leg in the following order: bugle bead, seed bead, bugle bead, seed bead, oval bead, seed bead, bugle bead, seed bead, bugle bead. Use the wire cutters to trim the excess wire from the end of each leg, leaving approximately ³⁄₁₆" (5 mm). Use the round-nose pliers to form a small loop at the end of each leg.

10. Adjust the legs, pincers, and tail as desired.

11. Thread the two 2" (5 cm) pieces of wire through two spacer bars and fold the wires down in one direction.

12. Place the two spacer bars over the exposed area where the leg wires were wrapped between spacer bars, pushing the folded wires down between the gaps in the spacer bars that make up the body of the scorpion. Turn the scorpion over and twist the wires in place, removing any excess wire

Finishing Touches

13. Use the wire cutters to trim two porcupine quills for the pincers and one porcupine quill for the stinger to just below the sharp point and at the widest point of the quill so that the trimmed piece is

Sand Garden

14. Remove any glass or paper from the picture frame. Keep the hard backing of the picture frame. Remove any hardware from the back of the frame.

15. With the picture frame face-down, apply a thin line of craft glue to the inside beveled portion of the frame. Lay the hard backing into the frame and press firmly around the edges to secure the backing to the frame and form a good seal. Allow to dry.

16. Turn the frame face up and fill the shallow opening with fine décor sand. Place a couple of smooth rocks in the sand, allowing space for the scorpion. Place the scorpion in the now-Zen garden wherever it looks best.

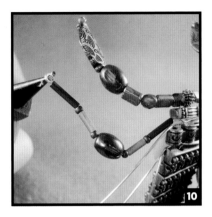

TRY THiS:

Use round toothpick tips instead of porcupine quills for the stinger and pincers. Paint them to match the scorpion. The 24-gauge wire is less sturdy, so don't pull the wires too snugly and risk snapping the wire that holds the scorpion's body intact.

approximately ½" (1.3 cm). Use a pin or needle to hollow out the inside of the trimmed portion of the quill in order to adhere the porcupine quill to the wire loop at the end of the pincers and tail. Place a small dab of E-6000 craft adhesive on the wire loops at the end of each pincer and the tail and push the porcupine quills over the wire loops. Set aside the scorpion to dry.

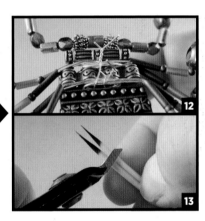

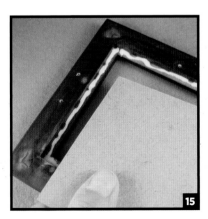

hermit crab
cage companion

*T*he hermit crab is not only the charming star of many boardwalk gift shops but now also a beaded mainstay. Abandoned or outgrown hermit crab shells can be put to a new use following these beading instructions.

SUPPLIES

» One 8" (20 cm) piece of 22-gauge wire
» Three 5" (13 cm) pieces of 22-gauge wire
» One 2" (5 cm) piece of 22-gauge wire
» One medium-size beginner hermit crab shell with thin membrane
» One heart bead
» One 25-mm focal bead
» One 15-mm oval or tube bead
» Sixteen seed beads
» Two teardrop seed beads
» Six bugle beads
» Six 12-mm oval beads
» Six 28-mm flat oval beads
» Alligator clip
» E-6000 craft adhesive

TOOLS

» Wire cutters
» Round-nose pliers
» Flat-nose pliers
» Rotary tool with 1/16" (1.6 mm) drill bit

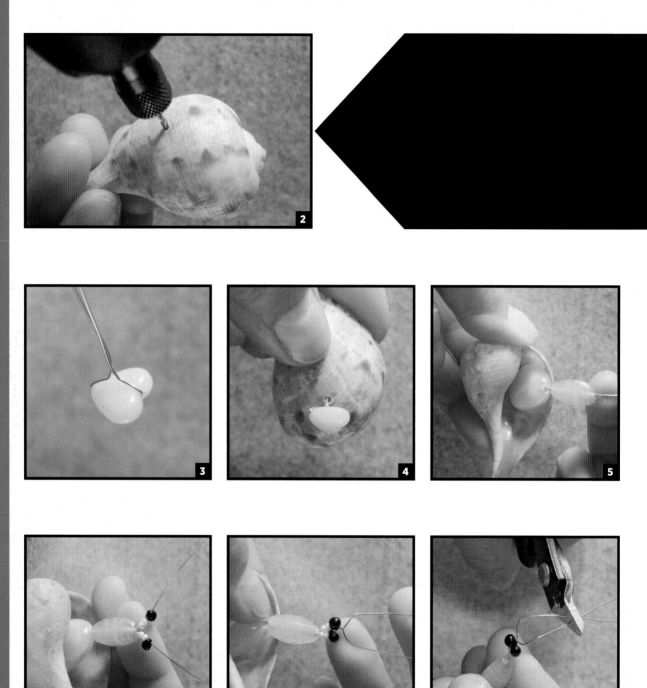

1. Cut the pieces of wire that will be used for this project. The 8" (20 cm) piece of wire is used for the body of the hermit crab. The three 5" (13 cm) pieces of wire are used for the legs of the hermit crab. The 2" (5 cm) piece of wire is used for the hermit crab's antennae.

Shell
· · · · · · · · ·

2. Use the rotary tool with the ¹⁄₁₆" (1.6 mm) drill bit to drill a hole through the top back of the "hood" of the opening of the shell, which is directly above the spiral part of the shell.

3. Thread the heart bead onto the center of the 8" (20 cm) piece of wire. Use the flat-nose pliers or your fingers to pinch the wire closed at the flat back of the heart bead.

4. Thread the two wires through the hole in the shell from the outside.

Abdomen, Antennae & Eyes
· · · · · · · · · · · · · · · · · · · ·

5. Thread the 25-mm focal bead onto the two wires followed by the 15-mm oval or tube bead.

6. Spread the two wires apart at the end of the 15-mm oval or tube bead, and thread two seed beads and one teardrop seed bead on each wire.

7. Twist the two pieces of wire together at the end of the two teardrop seed beads.

8. Trim the excess wire to approximately ½" (1 cm). Bend the remaining wires slightly so that they resemble the hermit crab's antennae.

Legs

9. Holding the three pieces of 5" (13 cm) wire together, wrap the pieces around the folded wire between the 25-mm focal bead and the 15-mm oval or tube bead starting from the top, crisscrossing underneath, and bringing the six legs back to the front.

10. Thread the following beads onto the first leg (start with any leg): bugle bead, seed bead, 12-mm oval bead, seed bead, 28-mm flat oval bead.

11. Using the wire cutters, trim the excess wire to approximately ³⁄₁₆" (5 mm) remaining wire.

12. Using the round-nose pliers, form a loop at the end of the leg. Continue beading the other five legs following Steps 10–12.

13. Gently bend each leg between the oval bead and the flat oval bead.

Finishing Touches

14. Wrap the 2" (5 cm) piece of wire around the folded wire between the beaded eyes and the 15-mm oval or tube bead starting from the top, crisscrossing underneath, and bringing the two ends back to the front. Trim the wires so that they are even, and bend them to resemble the hermit crab's other antennae.

15. Apply a pea-size amount of E-6000 craft adhesive to the top of the 25-mm focal bead and push the glued area against the underside of the hood of the shell. Turn the shell upside down, if necessary, to keep the glued area in place, and allow to dry. This will provide more stability to the hermit crab's body.

16. When the glue has dried, apply a short line of E-6000 adhesive to the underside of the crab's body (not the shell). Carefully place an alligator clip long side down with teeth pointing in the direction of the crab's head. Make sure the alligator clip is as close to the head and eyes of the crab as possible so that when it dries, it will be easy to clip the hermit crab to an edge or surface.

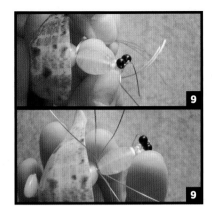

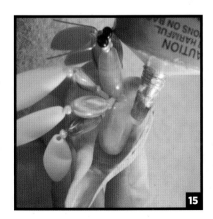

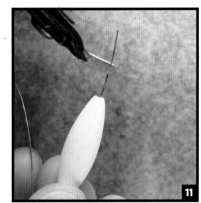

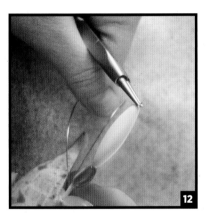

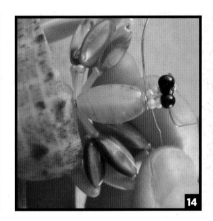

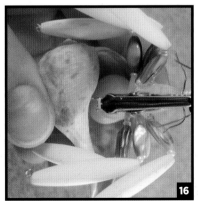

TRY THiS:

Add a bugle bead to each antenna wire and use the round-nose pliers to create a loop for more substantial antennae.

fireflies
in a jar

*N*ow you don't have to wait for summertime to enjoy catching fireflies. This jar of glow-in-the dark lightning bugs can be enjoyed year-round.

MATERIALS

SUPPLIES

» One glass quart jar with lid
» 4-petal metal bead cap (makes two fireflies)
» Two 8-mm plastic glow beads (see Resources, page 128)
» Two 4-mm plastic glow beads (see Resources, page 128)
» One 5-mm plastic glow bead (see Resources, page 128)
» One 6-mm plastic glow bead (see Resources, page 128)
» Twelve lime green seed beads
» Two coral or orange E beads
» One black E bead

» One 7" (17.8 cm) piece of light green 28-gauge floral wire for body
» One 8" (20 cm) piece of light green 28-gauge floral wire for wings and two legs
» Three 2" (5 cm) pieces of light green 28-gauge floral wire for legs
» Antique-finish bronze metallic paint
» Primer and clear sealer
» Yellow or lime green acrylic paint
» E-6000 craft adhesive

TOOLS

» Wire cutters
» Fine-tip paintbrush

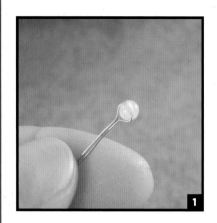

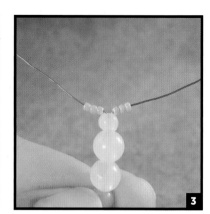

4. Thread the following beads onto one piece of wire in the following order: coral/orange E bead, black E bead, coral/orange E bead. Arch both wires inward, and put the wire without the E beads through the three E beads. Pull both wire

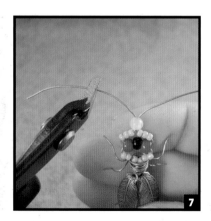

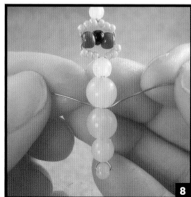

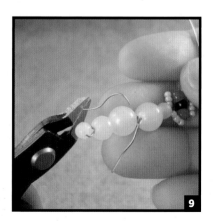

Abdomen, Thorax & Head

1. Thread one 4-mm glow bead halfway onto the 7" (18 cm) piece of wire. Fold the wire in half and pinch the wire together next to the bead.

2. Thread the following beads onto both pieces of wire in the following order: one 6-mm glow bead, two 8-mm glow beads, one 5-mm glow bead. Spread apart the two pieces of wire.

3. Thread three lime green seed beads onto each piece of wire.

ends tightly so that the three E beads are centered over the six lime green seed beads.

5. Thread three more lime green seed beads onto each wire. Then pinch the two wires together and

twist them once so that the twist is centered over the black seed bead.

6. Thread the other 4-mm glow bead onto the twisted wires and push down over the twist in the wire.

TRY THIS:

Add real blinking lights to the jar with small, battery-operated string lights that have a pendant loop for easy hanging.

7. Trim the excess wire evenly to about ½" (1 cm) and arch the wires outward to form the antennae.

Back Legs

8. Wrap one 2" (5 cm) piece of wire around and between the two 8-mm glow beads.

9. Trim the excess wire back to ½" (1 cm) on both sides to form the firefly's back legs. Bend the legs to preferred angles.

Wings

10. Open the petal-shaped prongs of the metal bead cap. Use the wire cutters to cut through the center of the bead cap so that each leftover piece has two petals.

11. Fold the 8" (20 cm) piece of wire in half and place one of the two-petal bead cap remnants (the wings) in the fold of the wire so that the wire goes between the two petals. Twist the wire once around the top of the wings.

12. Adjust the wings so that they lie flat against the length of the beaded body and the top of the wings is nestled between the 5- and 8-mm glow beads. Wrap the leftover wire around both sides of

Front Legs

13. Trim wires to ½" (1 cm) long. These are two of the firefly's front legs. Bend them to preferred angles. Wrap the other 2" (5 cm) piece of wire around the wire-wrapped portion of the firefly, crisscross the wire underneath, and bring the wire back up on both sides of the firefly's body. Trim wire to ½" (1.5 cm) on both sides. Bend these last two legs to preferred angles.

Finishing Touches

14. Apply E-6000 craft adhesive to the glow beads under the wings to keep the wings in place.

16. Use the fine-tip paint brush to paint the edges of the wings with light green or yellow acrylic paint. Allow to dry.

17. Use the fine-tip paint brush to apply primer and sealer to keep the paint from chipping off the wings.

18. Glue the fireflies to the inside of a jar in a random pattern, or wrap their legs around twigs or branches and insert them into the jar. Replace the jar lid. Place the jar of fireflies near a bright light or black light source for several minutes. Then turn off the lights and enjoy your creation.

the beaded body between the glow beads until approximately ½" (1 cm) of wire is left on both sides and the excess wire comes from underneath the firefly's body.

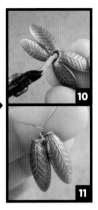

15. Using the fine-tip paint brush, paint the wings with antique-finish metallic paint. Allow to dry.

bug-eye
fishing jig

Colorful beads and feathers can be paired with all-purpose fish hooks to attract small fish or to add some splash to a lucky fishing hat.

MATERIALS

SUPPLIES
» One small glass eye bead
» One similar-size coordinating glass bead
» One small colorful feather plume
» One bobber stop
» One size-8 plain all-purpose fish hook
» One standard eye pin

TOOLS
» Flat-nose pliers
» Wire cutters
» Round-nose pliers
» Scissors

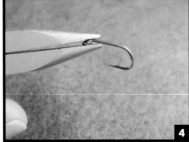

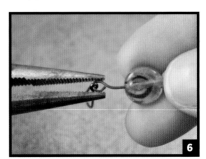

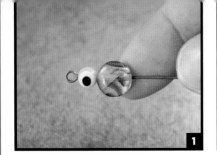

1. Thread the small eye bead and then the coordinating glass bead onto the eye pin.

2. Use wire cutters to trim the eye pin wire so that approximately ½" (1 cm) remains.

3. Use round-nose pliers to form a loop big enough so that a fish hook will fit loosely inside. Leave the loop open to attach the hook.

4. Use flat-nose pliers to pinch the looped end of the fish hook so that it is flat instead of slightly curved.

5. Slide the fish hook onto the loop.

6. Close the loop with the flat-nose pliers.

TRY THiS:

Instead of brightly colored bobber stops, use 6-lb.-test transparent fishing line to tie an overhand knot with at least four loops to secure the fish hook and feather.

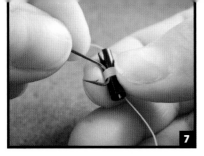

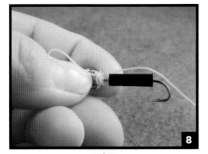

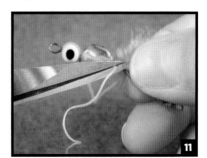

7. Slide the hook into the black tube of the bobber stop and under the wrapped thread so that the tube covers the loop holding the hook.

8. Slide the wrapped thread off the black tube and onto the eye pin close to the bottom bead.

9. Insert a feather (trimmed to about the length of the fish hook so that it just covers the hook when dangling) through the wrapped thread. If the bottom bead hole is big enough, try to insert the feather into the hole to keep it in place for the next step.

10. When the feather is in place, pull both ends of the bobber stop thread tightly so that it secures the feather to the eye pin. Use two pairs of flat-nose pliers if necessary to ensure a tight fit.

11. Trim off the excess bobber stop thread using a pair of scissors.

butterfly
lamp finial

A butterfly lamp finial is a great way to bring nature indoors to accessorize a simple lamp and give it color.

1. Cut the three pieces of wire needed for this project. The 7" (18 cm) piece of wire is used for the body, the 30" (76 cm) piece of wire is for the beaded wing centers, and the 18" (46 cm) piece of wire is used for the outer edge of the wings.

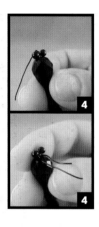

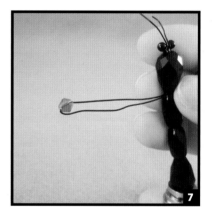

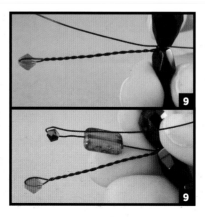

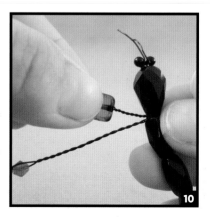

DIRECTIONS

Thorax

2. Fold the 7" (18 cm) piece of wire in half, and thread the spacer bead onto the center of the wire. Push both wires through the bottom of the lamp finial until they cannot be pulled any farther.

3. Thread four 14-mm black beads onto both wires. Spread the wires apart above the top bead.

4. Thread a 3.4-mm black drop bead onto each wire. Fold each wire down, wrap the wire around to the front, and bring the wires up through the center where the drop beads connect to make the antennae.

5. Trim the antennae evenly to about ½" (1.5 cm).

Inner Wings

6. Find the center of the 30" (76 cm) piece of wire by folding it in half. Place the fold between the first and second bead down from the antennae, wrap the wire around to the back of the butterfly body, crisscross the wire in back, and bring the wire back to the front. Pull the wires gently to secure the wire around the butterfly body.

7. Starting with one side of the butterfly, slide one bead (in this case an orange bicone bead) onto the wire. Place the bead approximately 1½" (4 cm) from the start of the wire and fold the wire back in toward the butterfly body with the bead at the fold.

8. Grasp the bead between two fingers and hold the two wires together while twisting the bead so that the whole length of the two wires are twisted together.

9. Wrap the excess wire around the back and pull it to the side again to continue beading and twisting wires. This time fold the wire at about the 1¼" (3 cm) mark or place the bead just short of where the last beaded strand is, folding the wire back, and twisting.

10. Consider adding more than one bead to the wire for each twisted strand. To twist more than one bead on the same strand, start by twisting the bead at the fold while holding the two wires together at the next bead to keep the strand from pushing the next bead down during the twisting process. Then, start twisting the second bead while holding the two wires together at the base of the butterfly body until the two wires are twisted firmly together all the way down the strand.

11. Continue twisting strands so that each upper wing has approximately four strands. When enough strands have been completed, pull the excess wire around to the back of the butterfly body, wrap it once more around the body of the butterfly (or around the base of the strands), and trim off all excess wire.

13. Continue twisting strands so that each lower wing has approximately three strands. When enough strands have been completed, pull the excess wire around to the back of the butterfly body, wrap it once more around the body of the butterfly (or around the base of the completed strands), and trim off all excess wire.

Outer Wings

14. Find the center of the other 18" (46 cm) piece of wire by folding it in half. Place the fold between the first and second bead down from the antennae, wrap the wire around to the back of the butterfly body, criss-cross the wire in back, and bring the wire back to the front. Pull the wires gently to secure around the butterfly body.

16. Wrap the wire around the center of the butterfly (between the second and third beads), and wrap it one more time to hold it in place.

17. Continue beading the wire for the outer edge of the lower wing. Fasten the wire end by wrapping it twice between the third and fourth beads of the butterfly body and trim the excess wire at the back of the butterfly.

18. Continue beading the wing outer edges of the other side of the butterfly and trim and fasten the wire as described in Steps 14–17.

12. As with Steps 6–11, find the center of one 18" (46 cm) piece of wire by folding it in half. Place the fold between the second and third bead down from the antennae, wrap the wire around to the back of the butterfly body, cross the wire in back, and bring the wire back to the front. Pull the wires gently to secure the wire around the butterfly body.

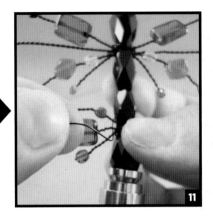

15. Begin with one wire, and thread black and orange seed beads in a random pattern until the beaded wire is long enough to loop around the outside of the clustered bead design at the center of the wing.

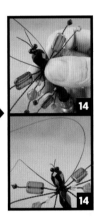

Finishing Touches

19. Apply E-6000 craft adhesive to the wired areas of the back of the butterfly body to keep loose ends from coming undone.

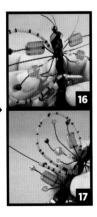

fly tie tack

*T*he bothersome housefly is now a beautiful and subtly humorous tie tack and will most certainly be a hot topic at the water cooler.

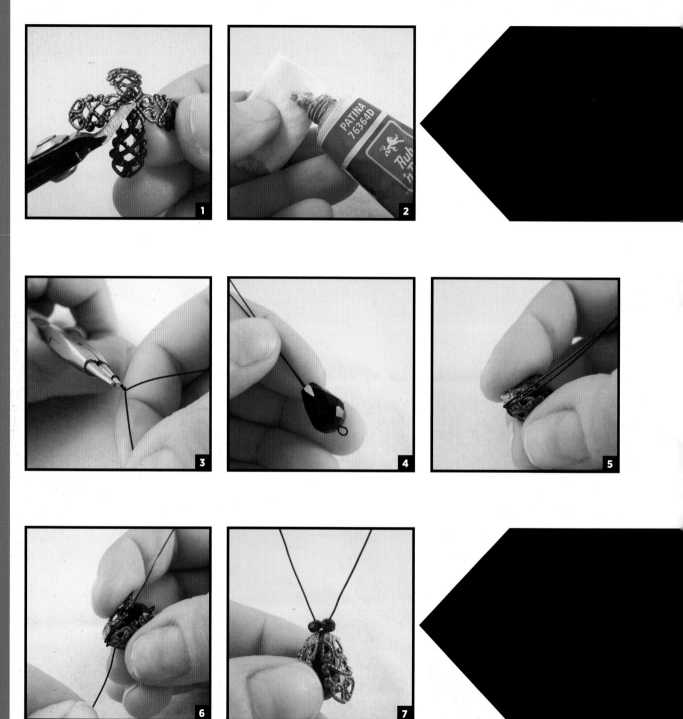

Wings

1. Pry apart the petals of the filigree bead cap, and use the wire cutters to cut through the center of the bead cap, creating two sets of wings.

2. Apply a dot of patina to a small square of paper towel, and rub it over the surface of the wings until the wings have the desired aged look.

Abdomen & Thorax

3. Fold the 6" (15 cm) piece of wire in half. Place the round-nose pliers in the folded notch and twist the two wires together to form a loop.

4. Thread the 13-mm oval or teardrop bead onto both pieces of wire.

Eyes

5. Fold the two pieces of wire down over the center top of the wings.

6. One at a time, pull each wire under a wing and back up toward the head of the fly.

7. Thread a 2-mm bicone bead onto each wire.

TRY THiS:

Cufflink bases can be found through jewelry supply distributors and online. Make matching cufflinks to go with the fly tie tack.

Legs

8. Fold the wires down along each side of the fly eyes, crisscross underneath the fly, and bring back to the top of the fly between the eyes and the wings/teardrop bead. Bend the legs to resemble a real fly.

9. Trim the fly legs to approximately ½" (1 cm).

10. Slide the two 2" (5 cm) pieces of wire up between the wings and the teardrop bead toward the eyes of the fly. Cross the legs under the fly and bring them back toward the top of the fly.

11. Place a small dot of E-6000 craft adhesive where the wires cross underneath the fly to keep the wires stable before adjusting and trimming the other four legs.

12. When the glue has dried, use the wire cutters to trim the other four legs back to approximately ½" (1 cm).

13. Use the flat-nose pliers to bend the last four legs to resemble a real fly.

Finishing Touches

14. Apply a small dot of E-6000 craft adhesive to the center of the teardrop bead.

15. Adhere the tie tack base to the glued area of the teardrop bead and allow to dry.

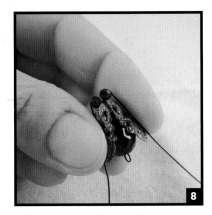

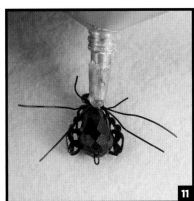

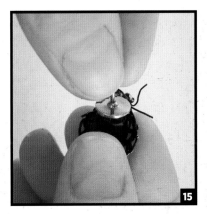

bat mobile

*I*t doesn't need to be Halloween to add this dark decoration to the corner of a room. The bat mobile will give any nook a downright creepy feel, and sparkly, patterned wings are a surprising touch to the otherwise simple design.

MATERIALS

SUPPLIES FOR BAT
Note: Supplies are for one beaded bat.

» One 5" (13 cm) piece of 1 ½" (4 cm) wide wire-edged black ribbon
» Black glitter clearcoat
» One 9" (23 cm) piece of 28-gauge black wire
» Two 11-mm black oval beads
» One 9-mm black barrel bead
» One 11-mm black flat oval bead
» Two #3 black bugle beads
» One 19-mm black focal bead
» Two 8-mm black flat diamond beads
» E-6000 craft adhesive
» 6-lb.-test fishing line

SUPPLIES FOR MOBILE
Note: Supplies are for three arcs that hold a total of five bats.

» Approximately 10 to 30 black and gray beads in various sizes
» Two 15" (38 cm) pieces of 18-gauge black wire
» One 18" (46 cm) piece of 12-gauge black wire

TOOLS

» White chalk pencil
» Scissors
» Wire cutters
» Round-nose pliers

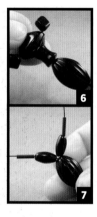

1

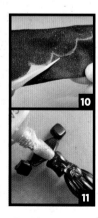

2

3

4

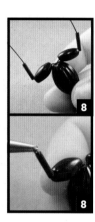

5

Bat Head

1. Use the wire cutters to cut the wire needed for the bat's body. Slide the following beads onto the center of the wire: one 8-mm flat diamond bead, one 11-mm flat oval bead, one 8-mm flat diamond bead.

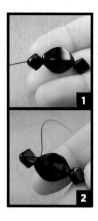

6

7

8

8

9

Bat Body & Legs

6. Thread beads onto the two pieces of wire in the following order: one 9-mm barrel bead, one 19-mm focal bead.

10

11

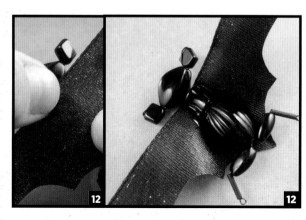

12

12

13

2. Starting at one end with a flat diamond bead, fold the wire toward the threaded beads and press it against the back of the 8-mm flat diamond bead.

3. Hold the wire in place against the 8-mm flat diamond bead with one hand, and wrap the wire twice around the space between the 8-mm flat diamond bead and the 11-mm flat oval bead.

4. Ensuring that the beads stay tightly centered on the wire, repeat this process with the 8-mm flat diamond bead on the other side. Twist and point the bat's ears up.

5. Both remaining wires should point in the same direction. Twist together the two pieces of excess wire so that the wire is tight against the side of the 11-mm flat oval bead. The head of the bat is now complete.

7. Spread the wires apart and thread beads onto each leg wire in the following order: one 11-mm oval bead, one #3 bugle bead.

8. Bend the legs. Use the wire cutters to trim the excess wire on each leg, leaving approximately 3/16" (5 mm). Use the round-nose pliers to create a loop to finish each leg.

Bat Wings

9. Fold the 5" (13 cm) piece of wire-edged ribbon in half. Use a white chalk or watercolor pencil to draw scallops for the wings from the bottom of the fold to the opposite, upper corner of the ribbon.

10. Use the scissors to cut out the wings along the chalk lines. Open the wings and press flat.

11. Place a small line of craft adhesive on the outside middle of the bat's back.

12. Press the bat wings into place at the center of the bat so that the pointed centers of the wings face the tail of the bat. Allow to dry.

13. Create a loose fold at the top edge of each bat wing to resemble the shape of a bat wing in flight.

Mobile

14. Use the wire cutters to cut the pieces of wire needed for arcs of the mobile. The 18" (46 cm) piece of 12-gauge wire is for the top piece of the mobile. The two 15" (38 cm) pieces of 18-gauge wire will hang from the main piece of the mobile with one bat on each end.

15. For each piece of wire, find the center of the wire with a pencil and wrap the wire around the pencil so that the two long pieces of wire cross over one another.

16. Continue to wrap each piece of wire one more time around the pencil to create a clover shape.

17. Twist the two wire ends together at the base of the clover design and separate the wires.

18. Starting with each 15" (38 cm) piece of 18-gauge wire, begin to thread a mix of black and gray beads onto each end of wire until approximately ½" (1 cm) of wire is left. Use the round-nose pliers to create a loop at each end.

19. At each end of the 18" (46 cm) piece of 12-gauge wire, use the round-nose pliers to create a loop. No beads are threaded onto this arc. Slide the top loop of the clover design of each 15" (38 cm) beaded arc into the loop that was created at each end of the 18" (46 cm) unbeaded arc, and close each loop.

20. Tie varying lengths of 6-lb.-test fishing line to a bat and to the loops at the end of the 15" (38 cm) beaded arcs and the center of the clover on the main 18" (46 cm) unbeaded arc.

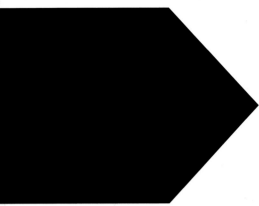

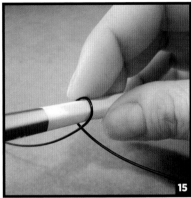

15

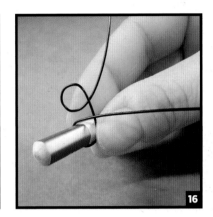

16

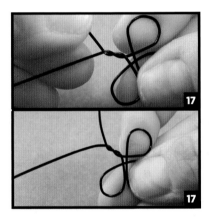

17

17

18

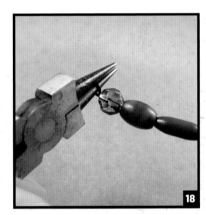

18

19

20

TRY THiS:

Any ribbon wider than 1½" (4 cm) can be used for this project. Just trace the wings to the 1½" (4 cm) width point. Use polka-dot or striped ribbon for less-conventional bat wings.

Tie fishing line around the bats' necks to make them all face the same direction, or vary where on the bat's body you tie the line to make them appear as if they are flitting in different directions.

praying mantis
terrarium figurine

*T*he praying mantis is a fascinating insect known to eat creatures as large as snakes and rodents, but this beaded version is perfectly harmless.

MATERIALS

SUPPLIES

» One 10" (25 cm) piece of 26-gauge green wire

» One 2 ½" (6.5 cm) piece of 22-gauge green wire

» One 7" (18 cm) piece of 26-gauge green wire

» Two 5" (13 cm) pieces of 26-gauge green wire

» One 12-mm triangular or heart-shaped green bead

» Two 4-mm round light green or yellow beads

» One 22-mm green tube bead

» One 9-mm green round or round drop bead

» Two or three egg- or pear-shaped green beads with a combined measurement of 32 mm

» Four 20-mm green oval tube beads

» Twelve 13-mm green bugle beads

» Six 5-mm green bugle beads

» Twenty green seed beads

» Wire mesh

» Metallic green acrylic paint

» E-6000 craft adhesive

TOOLS

» Wire cutters

» Round-nose pliers

» Flat-nose pliers

» Fine-point felt-tip marker

» Scissors

» Paintbrush

DIRECTIONS

1. Use the wire cutters to cut the pieces of wire needed for this project. The 10" (25 cm) piece of 26-gauge wire is for the body of the mantis. The 2½" (6.5 cm) piece of 22-gauge wire is for the antennae. The three 5" (13 cm) and 7" (18 cm) pieces of 26-gauge wire are for the legs.

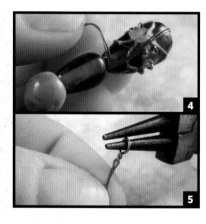

4. There are two options for finishing the wire at the end of the mantis's body: a) bend the excess wire lengths underneath the mantis's body and wrap/twist the wire between the first available space between beads, then

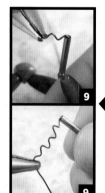

Legs

7. Wrap each of the three 26-gauge leg wires between the body beads: one 7" (18 cm) wire between the head and tube bead, one 5" (13 cm) wire between the tube and 9-mm

84

Head

2. Slide the 12-mm triangular or heart-shaped bead onto the 10" (25 cm) piece of 26-gauge wire. When the bead is centered on the wire, pinch the wires together near the widest part of the bead (the base of the triangle or the top of the heart). Twist the wire a couple of times to keep the two wires tight against the flat side of the bead.

Thorax & Abdomen

3. Thread these beads in the following order for the body of the mantis: one 22-mm tube bead, one 9-mm round or round drop bead, two or three egg- or pear-shaped beads measuring approximately 30 mm. Adjust the body so that the head tilts slightly down and the body bends at an approximately 60-degree angle.

trim the excess wire; or b) trim the wire back to approximately ³⁄₁₆" (5 mm) with the wire cutters, then use the round-nose pliers to loop both wires tightly against the last bead of the mantis's body.

Antennae

5. Use the round-nose pliers to create a small loop at the center of the 2 ½" (6.5 cm) piece of 22-gauge wire, and twist the wire once or twice around to secure the loop.

6. Thread both wires up through the bottom of the triangular or heart-shaped bead, and pry the wires apart at the top of the bead for the antennae. Trim the excess wire so that approximately ½" (1.5 cm) remains. Curve the wires to adjust the antennae as desired.

round or drop bead, and one 5" (13 cm) wire between the round or drop bead and the first egg- or pear-shaped bead. Starting with the wire at the underside, crisscross the wire over the top of the mantis and pull firmly so the ends stick straight out to the sides.

8. Thread beads on the legs between the triangular or heart-shaped bead and the 22-mm tube bead in the following order: one 13-mm bugle bead, one seed bead, one 20-mm oval tube bead, one seed bead, one 13-mm bugle bead.

9. Using wire cutters, trim the legs to 1" (2.5 cm). To create spikes on the underside of the forelegs, use the flat-nose pliers to bend the wire in a zigzag pattern to the length of the first 13-mm bugle bead.

→

10. Wrap the excess wire around the space between the first bugle bead and the seed bead once or twice. Use the wire cutters to completely trim off any excess wire. Press the zigzag piece of wire against the 13-mm bugle bead.

11. Thread beads on the legs between the 22-mm tube bead and the 9-mm round or round drop bead in the following order: one 20-mm oval tube bead, one seed bead, one 13-mm bugle bead, one seed bead, one 13-mm bugle bead.

12. Use the wire cutters to trim the excess wire, leaving 3/16" (5 mm). Use the round-nose pliers to create a loop to finish each leg.

seed bead, one #3 bugle bead, one seed bead, one #3 bugle bead.

14. Use the wire cutters to trim the excess wire, leaving 3/16" (5 mm). Use the round-nose pliers to create a loop to finish each leg.

Wings

15. Fold the 1 1/4" x 2" (3 x 5 cm) piece of wire mesh in half the long way. Use a felt-tip marker to draw a wing onto the mesh, making sure the fold is along the top outside edge of the wing. The length of the wings should match the measured length of the combined egg- or pear-shaped beads at the end of the mantis.

16. Use the scissors to cut out the wings, making sure not to cut through the fold.

18. Use a paintbrush to apply a layer of metallic green paint onto the mesh wings. Allow to dry.

19. Apply a small line of E-6000 craft adhesive to the underside of the wings, and press the wings into place. Allow to dry.

Eyes

20. Add a small dot of E-6000 craft adhesive to either side of the triangular or heart-shaped bead, and place the 4-mm round beads on either side so that each bead hole faces out to resemble the mantis's pupils. Allow to dry.

13. Thread beads on the legs between the 9-mm round or round drop bead and the first egg- or pear-shaped bead in the following order: one 13-mm bugle bead, two seed beads, one 13-mm bugle bead, two seed beads, one #3 bugle bead, one

10

10

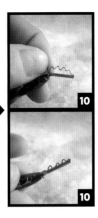

11

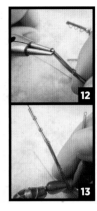

12

13

17. Open the wings. Create an accordian-style fold at the center of the wings. Shape the wings over the back of the mantis to be sure that they drape well.

15

16

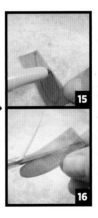

17

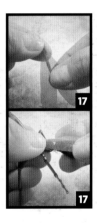

17

17

18

19

19

20

TRY THiS:

Instead of the green beads recommended for this project, use beads in shades of brown—even wooden beads—to resemble other mantises in nature.

picnic ant
magnet

*T*his larger version of the average ant is a much more acceptable visitor in the kitchen. Decorate a refrigerator door with an army of these not-so-pesky critters.

MATERIALS

SUPPLIES

Note: Supplies are for making one picnic ant.

- » One 5" (13 cm) piece of 28-gauge wire
- » Three 4" (10 cm) pieces of 28-gauge wire
- » One 16-mm flat oval bead
- » One 12-mm heart-shaped bead
- » Two 4-mm round beads
- » Two 3-mm spacer beads
- » Twelve 3-mm bugle beads
- » Six #3 bugle beads
- » Nineteen seed beads
- » ¼" x ⅞" (6 mm x 2.2 cm) ceramic block magnet
- » E-6000 craft adhesive

TOOLS

- » Wire cutters
- » Round-nose pliers

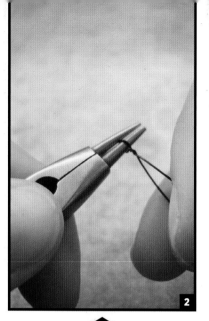

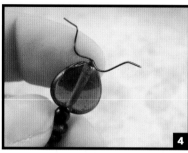

1. Use the wire cutters to cut the pieces of wire needed for this project. The 5" (13 cm) piece of wire is for the ant's body. The 4" (10 cm) pieces of wire are for the ant's legs.

Abdomen, Thorax & Head

2. Fold the 5" (13 cm) piece of wire in half, and use the round-nose pliers to twist a very small loop at the center of the wire. Twist it twice, and then straighten the wires.

3. Thread the beads for the ant's body in the following order: flat oval bead, round bead, spacer bead, spacer bead, round bead, heart-shaped bead (widest end first).

4. Trim the excess wire, leaving two pieces of 1" (2.5 cm) wire. Slide a seed bead onto both wires and push tightly against the heart-shaped bead. Spread the two wires apart, and shape them to resemble ant antennae.

Legs

5. One at a time, wrap each of the three 4" (10 cm) pieces of wire: one between a round and spacer bead, one between the two spacer beads, and one between the other spacer and round bead. Starting with the wire at the top of the ant, crisscross the wire underneath the ant and bring the wires up toward the top of the ant. Pull each wire firmly in place.

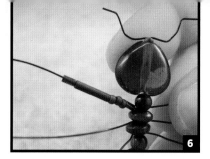

6. One leg at a time, thread the leg beads in the following order: one 3-mm bugle bead, three seed beads, one #3 bugle bead, one 3-mm bugle bead.

7. Use the wire cutters to trim the excess wire, leaving approximately 3/16" (5 mm) of wire. Use the round-nose pliers to create a small loop at the end of the leg.

8. Adjust the legs of the ant to resemble a real ant. Adjust the body so that the middle of the ant dips down and comes back up in a U shape and the head and end beads tilt downward from the center of the ant.

Finishing Touches

9. Apply a small amount of E-6000 craft adhesive to the underside of the ant, and glue the magnet in place so that the magnet is mostly hidden by the ant's body.

TRY THiS:

If red or brown spacer beads are difficult to find, look for wooden spacers and simply paint them the desired color.

honeybee
tea infuser

*T*ea infusers have such potential for embellishment with beads and charms, and this honeybee finish will create quite a buzz.

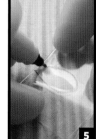

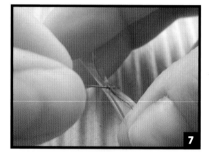

Tea Infuser

1. Use the wire cutters to remove the chain from the strainer ball. Remove hook with flat-nose pliers and set it aside.

2. Thread a mixture of desired beads onto one eye pin, leaving about ⅜" (9 mm) of remaining wire. Use the round-nose pliers to create a loop, but leave the loop slightly open. Hook the open loop into the metal loop of the strainer ball, and close it with flat-nose pliers.

3. Thread another set of beads, or the teapot or another pendant and the 9-mm round bead (if chosen), onto an eye pin, leaving about ⅜" (9 mm) of wire. Use wire cutters to trim excess wire if necessary. Use the round-nose pliers to create a loop, but leave it slightly open.

4. Hook the 1" (2.5 cm) piece of bead-linked chain in the open loop of the teapot-beaded eye pin, and use the flat-nose pliers to close the loop.

Bee Wings

5. Fold the piece of heavy clear vinyl in half the long way (¾" [2 cm] end to ¾" end). Trace a rounded wing on the vinyl with a fine-point marker, making sure the center of the wings is on the fold.

6. Keeping the vinyl folded, cut out the wings with scissors.

7. Use a needle to create two holes through the bee wings: one through the lower section of the center and one through the upper section of the center.

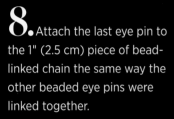

Bee Abdomen, Thorax, Wings & Head

8. Attach the last eye pin to the 1" (2.5 cm) piece of bead-linked chain the same way the other beaded eye pins were linked together.

9. Thread beads onto the last eye pin in the following order: one 12-mm yellow pear-shaped or drop bead, one 2-mm black disk bead, one 5-mm yellow round or diamond-shaped bead, vinyl bee wings, one black E bead. Use the wire cutters to trim the excess wire back to ⅜" (9 mm), and use the round-nose pliers to create a loop.

Bee Legs

10. Wrap one 2" (5 cm) piece of 20-gauge wire between the E bead and wings starting from the top of the bee, criss-crossing underneath the bee, and bringing the wire back up to the top. Trim the excess wire to ⅝" (1.6 cm) and angle the legs.

11. Continue wrapping the other 2" (5 cm) pieces of wire as in Step 10, one above the black spacer bead and one below the black spacer bead.

Finishing Touches

12. Place the hook from the tea infuser chain through the loop at the head of the bee, and pinch the hook closed with the flat-nose pliers.

13. Apply E-6000 craft adhesive to the underside of the bee to secure wires and beads.

stick insect
hat pin

*W*alking stick bugs vary widely in nature, so this project is perfect for experimentation with bead color and shape.

SUPPLIES

» One 10" (25 cm) piece of 26-gauge wire
» Three 7" (18 cm) pieces of 20-gauge wire
» One 1½" (4 cm) brown horn bead
» Five 4-mm round brown beads
» One 5-mm bicone brown bead
» Thirty-two brown seed beads
» Thirty 7-mm brown bugle beads
» Twelve 9-mm brown bugle beads

» One stick pin with ¾" (2 cm) glue pad (see Resources, page 128)
» One stick pin clutch (see Resources, page 128)
» Acrylic sealer
» Craft adhesive

TOOLS

» Wire cutters
» Round-nose pliers
» Brown fine-point marker (optional)

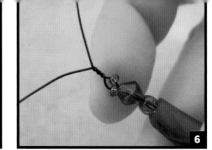

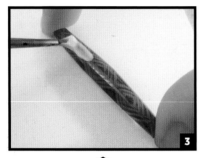

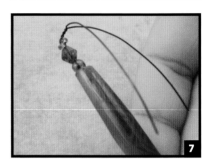

1. Use the wire cutters to cut the pieces of wire needed for this project: the 10" (25 cm) piece of 28-gauge wire is for the body and antennae of the bug, and the three 7" (18 cm) pieces of 20-gauge wire are for the legs.

Body

2. Use the marker to draw a design on the 1 ½" (4 cm) brown horn bead.

3. Paint a thin coat of sealer over the design on the horn bead. Allow to dry.

4. Slide one 4-mm round brown bead onto the center of the 10" (25 cm) piece of wire. Pinch the wire closed and tightly twist it twice close to the bead.

5. Thread the following beads onto both pieces of wire in the following order: three 4-mm round brown beads, the brown horn bead, one 4-mm round brown bead, one 5-mm bicone brown bead. Separate the two wires.

6. Thread one seed bead onto each wire. Twist the two wires together two or three times.

7. Bend the antennae wires back toward the body of the bug.

TRY THiS:

The walking stick bug would undoubtedly also be at home in a terrarium.

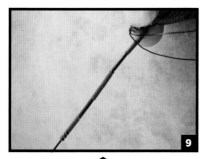

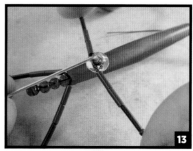

Legs

8. Wrap one 7" (18 cm) piece of 20-gauge wire between the 5-mm bicone brown bead and 4-mm round brown bead starting from the top of the bug, crisscrossing underneath the bug, and bringing the legs back up.

9. Thread the following beads onto each leg in this order: two 7-mm bugle beads, one 9-mm bugle bead, one seed bead, two 7-mm bugle beads, one 9-mm bugle bead, one seed bead, one 7-mm bugle bead, three seed beads.

10. Use the wire cutters to trim the excess wire back to ¼" (6 mm), and use the round-nose pliers to create a loop at the end of each leg.

11. Wrap one 7" (18 cm) piece of 20-gauge wire around the bend in the stick pin where it connects to the glue pad. Apply E-6000 craft adhesive to the twist in the wire on the outside of the glue pad to secure the wire to the glue pad. Allow to dry.

12. Wrap the last 7" (18 cm) piece of 20-gauge wire between the bottom of the brown horn bead and the 4-mm round brown bead right next to it. Continue threading beads onto the back two legs following Step 9.

13. Thread beads onto the two pieces of wire wrapped around the stick pin following Step 9. Then apply E-6000 craft adhesive to the glue pad and press the glue pad to the back of the horn bead approximately ½" (1 cm) above the back legs.

Book'mate' (-māt'), n. 1. A kind of

Book'mon'ger (-mŭn'gẽr), n. 1. A kind of

Book' mus'lin (-mŭz/lĭn), n. A kind of thin white muslin for la... dresses.
for the cov... A label, placed upon or in a ... library.

Book'plate' (-plāt'), n. A label, placed upon or in a book, showing its ownership or its position in a library.

Book'sell'er (-sĕl'ẽr), n. One who sells books.

Book'sell'ing, n. The employment of selling books.

Book'shelf' (-shĕlf'), n. ; pl. Bookshelves (-shĕlvz'). [Eng.] A shelf to hold books.

Book'shop' (-shŏp'), n. A bookseller's shop. [Eng.]

Book'stall' (-stal'), n. A stall ... stand where books are ... or stand for the ... ng or reference. ... ore where books are kept

Book'worm' (-wûrm'), n. 1. Work done upon a book newspaper or job work.

2. Study; application to books.

Book'worm' (-wûrm'), n. 1. (Zoöl.) Any larva of a beetle or moth, which is injurious to books. Many species are known.

2. A student closely attached to books ... addicted to study; a reader without appreciation. ... as mere a book-
I wanted but a bla... and a salary t... Pope.
worm as any the

Book'y (boo'k...) ... Bool'y (boo'lý) ... Boo'ly bo cow + g... cowherd; herdsmen, or a ... to place with f... like the Tart... inclos... for t... [Wr...

Bo... BEAM... purposes ... the jib bo...

2. (Mech.) A long spar or beam, project... the studding-sail boom, etc. ... ding the bottom ... a pa... A long pole o... ... ost of a derrick, from the outer end of ... is suspended. ... conspicuous top, set ... to mark ... [Obs.] ... le or line of

Boom'slang (Zöö... slang snake.] (Bucephalus Caper... by natives, it has s...

Boon (boon), n. bōn; akin to Sw... ban; but influen... See 2d BAN, Bo...
For which th...

2. That whi... vor; a gift; ... Every goo...

Boon, a. ous; as, b...

2. Kind...

Bo... coars... flax, ... by ... ge... to ... bar. See ... out for the ... r sail; as

bookworm
bookmark

A beaded bookmark nestles into the crease of any book and is a stylish and secure way to leave off a story.

SUPPLIES FOR BOOKWORM

» One 5" (10 cm) piece of 28-gauge wire
» Five 1 ½" (4 cm) pieces of 28-gauge wire
» One 3-mm round black bead
» One 6-mm round green bead
» Five 8-mm round green beads
» Ten 3-mm green disk or spacer beads
» Ten green seed beads
» Fifteen orange seed beads
» E-6000 craft adhesive

SUPPLIES FOR BOOKMARK

» One 9" (23 cm) length of 1-mm leather cord (Note: Measure the spine of a book and add 2" [5 cm])

» Two 3" (7.5 cm) pieces of 24- to 28-gauge wire
» Two jump rings
» One book charm (optional: eyeglasses charm)
» Various coordinating beads
» Two or three head pins
» One eye pin

TOOLS

» Wire cutters
» Round-nose pliers
» Flat-nose pliers

1. Use the wire cutters to cut the pieces of wire needed for this project: The 5" (10 cm) piece of 28-gauge wire is for the body of the bookworm; the five 1 ½" (4 cm) pieces of wire are for the book-

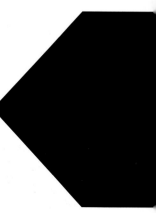

worm's legs; and the two 3" (7.5 cm) pieces of 24- to 28-gauge wire are for wrapping the ends of the leather cord.

Bookworm Body

2. Fold the 5" (13 cm) piece of 28-gauge wire in half. Thread the 3-mm black bead onto the center of the wire, and pinch the two wires together close to the bead.

3. Thread the following beads onto both wires in the following order: one 6-mm green bead, five 8-mm green beads.

4. Use the wire cutters to trim the excess wire so that approximately ¾" (2 cm) remains. Use the round-nose pliers to create two spirals. Then pinch the spirals close together. The two spirals create a sturdy loop for attaching the bookmark.

Bookworm Legs

5. Wrap each of the five 1½" (4 cm) pieces of 28-gauge wire between each of the round green beads starting at the bottom of the body, criss-crossing the wire at the top of the body, and pulling straight out to the sides, then down.

6. Thread the following beads onto each leg in the following order: one 3-mm green disk or spacer bead, one green seed bead, one orange seed bead.

7. Use the wire cutters to trim each leg wire to ⅛" (3 mm), and use the round-nose pliers to make a small tight loop against the orange seed bead.

Finishing Touch

8. Place a small dot of E-6000 craft adhesive on the top of each 8-mm round green bead, and place an orange seed bead centered on each green bead. Allow to dry.

The Bookmark

9. Use flat-nose pliers to twist open a jump ring, loop it through the spirals at the end of the bookworm, and close it again.

10. Put one end of the 9" (23 cm) piece of leather cord through the jump ring and fold 5/16" (8 mm) of the end piece against the cord.

11. Holding the fold, line up one end of a 3" (7.6 cm) piece of wire with the folded end of the leather cord, hold it along with the folded cord, and wrap the wire tightly around the folded cord starting at the jump ring and working toward the tip of the cord and wire, being sure to cover the ends.

12. Trim off excess wire, and press the wire against the cord with the flat-nose pliers.

13. Fold the opposite end of the leather cord through the other jump ring, and follow Step 10 for the bookmark to secure the opposite end with wrapped wire.

14. Thread various beads onto two or three head pins, finishing the ends by creating a loop with the round-nose pliers. These are used to create a cluster of beads at the opposite end of the bookmark from the bookworm.

15. Use the flat-nose pliers to open the eye pin and hook the book charm inside the loop before closing again. Thread various beads onto the eye pin, finishing the ends by creating a loop with the round-nose pliers.

16. Open the other jump ring as described in Step 9 of making the bookmark, and slide the head pin and eye pin loops onto the jump ring before closing it again.

9

9

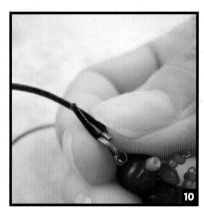

10

11

11

12

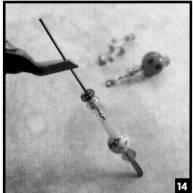

14

TRY THiS:

Give the bookworm a pair of wrapped-wire glasses. Experiment with a 1" (2.5 cm) piece of 28-gauge wire and the round-nose pliers. When the glasses look right, glue them in place.

15

15

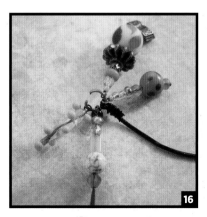

16

16

slug
hair comb

*E*very biology nerd should have this slug hair comb fashion accessory to proudly proclaim her fondness for even slimy members of the animal kingdom.

SUPPLIES

Note: Supplies are for one slug hair comb.

» One 6" (15 cm) piece of 28-gauge wire

» Two 6-mm eyeball beads

» Two #3 bugle beads

» Two 3-mm round beads

» Six graduated flat circle beads (ranging from approximately 10 mm to 16 mm)

» One 6-mm round bead

» One 12-mm tube bead

» 12" (30.5 cm) transparent stretchy jelly cord

» One hair comb

» E-6000 craft adhesive

TOOLS

» Wire cutters

» Round-nose pliers

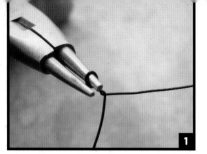

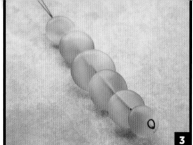

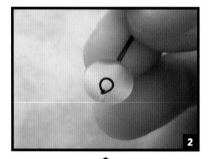

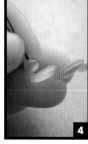

DIRECTIONS

Trunk

1. Fold the 6" (15 cm) piece of 28-gauge wire in half. Use the round-nose pliers to twist a small loop at the fold.

2. Thread the 10-mm flat circle bead onto both wires and push the loop flat against the bead.

3. Continue threading the following beads onto both pieces of wire in the following order: 12-mm flat circle bead, 13-mm flat circle bead, 16-mm flat circle bead, 13-mm flat circle bead, 12-mm flat circle bead.

Head

4. Bend the wires 90 degrees upward before threading the last two beads: the 6-mm round bead and the 12-mm tube bead. Spread the two wires apart.

Tentacles

5. Thread the following beads onto each slug tentacle: one 6-mm eyeball bead, one #3 bugle bead, one 3-mm round bead. (Optional: Place a dot of E-6000 craft adhesive between the eyeball beads to secure them in place so that the eyes don't swivel.)

6. Use the wire cutters to trim off the excess wire on each tentacle so that less than ¼" (6 mm) remains. Use the round-nose pliers to create a small loop tight against the 3-mm round bead.

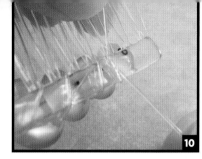

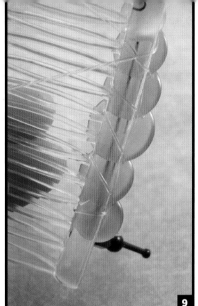

7. Push the loop at the end of each tentacle against the 3-mm round bead.

Hair Comb

8. Line up the clear stretchy cord along the side of the slug with approximately ½" (1.5 cm) of stretchy cord extending past the length of the slug. Loop the longest end twice around the space between the 12-mm flat circle bead and the 13-mm flat circle bead closest to the slug's eyes.

9. Center the slug on the top outside edge of the hair comb, tucking the short end of the stretchy cord between the comb tines closest to the tail end of the slug; then, start winding the jelly cord around and between the flat circle beads of the slug's body and the tines of the hair comb in a spiral motion until what was the longest end of the jelly cord meets up with the shortest end of the jelly cord.

10. Tie the two ends of jelly cord together in three tight knots, and trim off any excess.

TRY THiS:

Move the eye beads to the top and leave out the 3-mm round beads. Make more than one slug by doubling the supply list.

caged owl
tree topper

A *handmade whimsical tree topper adds just the right touch to a small decorative tree.*

SUPPLIES

- » Handmade lampwork owl bead (see Resources, page 128)
- » One 1" (2.5 cm) spacer bar with center hole
- » One head pin
- » Three 10" (25 cm) pieces of 26-gauge white-coated wire
- » Twelve 7" (17.8 cm) pieces of 26-gauge white-coated wire
- » One 5" (13 cm) piece of 26-gauge white-coated wire
- » One 3" (7.5 cm) piece of 26-gauge white-coated wire
- » Two 3" (7.5 cm) pieces of 26-gauge green-coated wire
- » One 14" (35.5 cm) piece of 26-gauge white-coated wire
- » One 1 ¾" (4.5 cm) wooden spool
- » One 5" (13 cm) length of ribbon
- » Six drop beads
- » Six jump rings
- » Six assorted 4-mm beads
- » Six pearl seed beads
- » Two flower beads
- » Two seed beads
- » Craft adhesive

TOOLS

- » Wire cutters
- » Round-nose pliers
- » Flat-nose pliers
- » Rotary tool with ⅟₁₆" (1.5 mm) drill bit

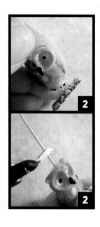
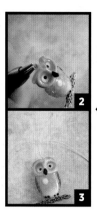

1. Cut the pieces of wire needed for this project. One of the 10" (25 cm) pieces of wire is for the perch. The twelve 7" (17.8 cm) pieces of wire are for the twisted vertical pieces of the cage. The 5" (13 cm) piece of wire is for securing the 7" (17.8 cm) pieces of wire together to form the top of the cage. The 3" (7.5 cm) piece of white-coated wire is to secure the perch to the top of the cage. The two 3" (7.5 cm) pieces of green-coated wire are for

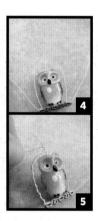
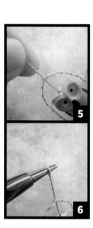
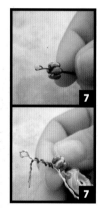

4. Thread each end of the 10" (25 cm) piece of wire through the two opposite ends of the spacer bar to form an arch over the owl. Bend the wires upward.

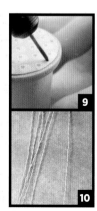
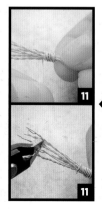

Cage

8. Trace around one end of the spool on a piece of decorative paper. Cut out the circle. Use craft adhesive to glue the circle to the top of the spool.

flower stems to twist around the perch. The 14" (35.5 cm) piece of wire is for the horizontal top looped section of the cage. The other two 10" (25 cm) pieces of wire are for the horizontal bottom sections of the cage.

Perch

2. Insert the head pin through the center of the spacer bar and slide the owl onto the head pin. Using wire cutters, trim the wire to ¼" (6 mm). Use the round-nose pliers to create a tight loop above the head.

3. Thread one 10" (25 cm) piece of wire through the loop above the owl's head until the owl is centered on the wire. Fold the wire in half and twist the wires tightly together up to ¼" (6 mm). Spread the wires apart to the sides.

5. Wind each wire back up around each side of the arch until the two wires meet at the center. Twist the wires together at the top of the perch for another ¼" (6 mm).

6. Use wire cutters to remove excess wire so that approximately ½" (1 cm) remains, and use the round-nose pliers to create a loop with the twisted perch wires.

7. Create flowers by folding the 3" (7.5 cm) pieces of green-coated wire in half, sliding a seed bead onto the center, then threading the wires through the center of a flower bead. Twist the stem wires together. Wrap the flower stem around the arch of the perch.

9. Mark six evenly spaced dots on the top of the spool for drilling holes for the vertical bird cage wires. Use the rotary tool to drill holes through the top edge of the spool at a 45-degree angle.

10. Two at a time, twist together the 7" (18 cm) pieces of wire from beginning to end.

11. Wrap the 5" (13 cm) piece of wire around all six twisted wire segments 1" (2.5 cm) from one end of the cluster of wires. Use the wire cutters to trim the short ends of the twisted wires so that they are all even.

→

12. Spread out the short ends of the twisted wires to form a six-pointed star shape. Use the round-nose pliers to curl each twisted wire segment under toward the wire cluster.

13. Spread out the long ends of the twisted wire segments so that they are evenly spaced, and apply E-6000 craft adhesive to the center of the wire cluster. Place the cluster inside of a cup to keep the segments spaced more evenly while the glue dries.

14. When the E-6000 craft adhesive has dried, thread the 3" (7.5 cm) piece of white-coated wire through the loop at the top of the owl perch so that one end of the wire is long enough to hold against the already-wrapped wire clusters and the long end of the wire can be

15. Thread each of the six twisted wire segments through the holes in the top of the spool until the owl is centered in the cage between the top and floor of the cage. Pull the twisted wire segments upward; then, loop them twice around themselves.

16. Thread each of the six assorted round beads onto each remaining piece of twisted wire segment; then, use the round-nose pliers to create a downward-facing loop at the end of each bead.

pinch it around the wire segment with the flat-nose pliers. Create a downward-facing loop centered between two of the twisted wire segments, and slide a pearl seed bead onto the wire so that the seed bead rests in the bottom of the loop; then, wind the long piece

of wire two times tightly around the next twisted wire segment. Continue this pattern all the way around the top of the birdcage, and wind the remaining wire around the twisted wire segment where the wire started. Use the wire cutters to remove any excess wire. Using the

photo on page 110 as a guide, wrap the other two 10" (25 cm) wires around the cage from one twisted segment to the next, this time omitting loops. One wire should be centered halfway down the cage, and the other near the bottom.

wrapped around the short end to secure the perch to the inside top of the bird cage. Bring the two wire ends up through opposite sides of the twisted wire segments (i.e., between each set of three twisted wire segments) to secure the perch in place and keep it balanced.

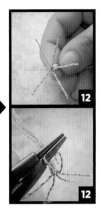
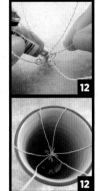

17. Place each of the six drop beads onto jump rings and hang the jump rings from each downward-facing spiral. Twist one end of the 14" (35.5 cm) piece of wire around one of the vertical twisted wire segments at the back of the cage, and

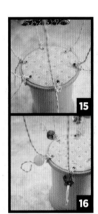

18. Place lines of craft adhesive covering one side of the 5" (13 cm) length of ribbon; then, place the ribbon glue side against the spool and wrap all the way around. Place a line of glue along the edge of the cut portion of the ribbon to keep it in place and from fraying.

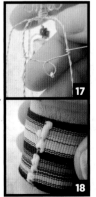

TRY THiS:

Use a heavier gauge for the vertical pieces of the cage and then wrap a light gauge of wire in spirals down the length of the vertical pieces for more intricate features. Add a tuft of colored cotton or glittery yarn to the bottom of the cage.

centipede
wiggler

*R*emove debris from any cool, dark, damp environment, and you'll likely find the wriggling and writhing centipede frantically seeking cover. Something about this leggy bug gives people a case of the heebie jeebies, so this sculptural project can be used for the element of surprise!

MATERIALS

SUPPLIES
» One 10" (25 cm) piece of 28-gauge wire
» Sixteen 2" (5 cm) pieces of 28-gauge wire
» Sixteen 8- x 5-mm brown disk beads
» Thirty-eight #3 bugle beads
» Ninety-six seed beads
» One black E bead

TOOLS
» Wire cutters
» Round-nose pliers

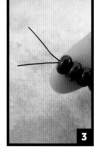

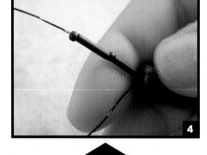

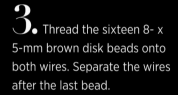

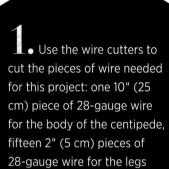

1. Use the wire cutters to cut the pieces of wire needed for this project: one 10" (25 cm) piece of 28-gauge wire for the body of the centipede, fifteen 2" (5 cm) pieces of 28-gauge wire for the legs of the centipede, and one 2" (5 cm) piece of 28-gauge wire for the antennae.

Body

2. Fold the 10" (25 cm) piece of wire in half. Thread the black E bead onto the center of the wire, and pinch the wire together below the E bead. This will be the head of the centipede.

3. Thread the sixteen 8- x 5-mm brown disk beads onto both wires. Separate the wires after the last bead.

4. The separated wires will be the centipede's hind leg. Thread the following beads onto each hind leg in this order: one bugle bead, one seed bead, one bugle bead, one seed bead.

5. Use the wire cutters to trim the two wires so that approximately ¼" (6 mm) remains. Use the round-nose pliers to make the smallest loop possible at the end of each wire so that there is as close to ¼" (6 mm) of space between the loop and the last threaded seed bead. This space is necessary for the wires that will be wrapped between each of the brown disk beads.

Legs

6. Begin wrapping each of the fifteen 2" (5 cm) pieces of wire between each of the

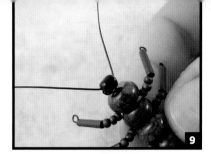

8- x 5-mm brown disk beads starting from the top of the centipede, crisscrossing the wire underneath the centipede, and bringing the wires back up toward the top of the centipede.

7. Thread the following beads onto each leg in the following order: three seed beads, one bugle bead. Use the wire cutters to trim the excess wire so that less than ¼" (6 mm) remains, and use the round-nose pliers to create a small loop tight against the bugle bead.

8. As each pair of legs is completed, adjust the legs so that they bend slightly between the third seed bead and

Antennae

9. Thread the last 2" (5 cm) piece of 28-gauge wire through the E bead at the head of the centipede so that the wires stick out evenly on both ends. These wires are the centipede's antennae.

10. Thread the following beads onto each antenna in the following order: one bugle bead, one seed bead, one bugle bead. Use the wire cutters to trim the excess wire from both antennae so that less than ¼" (6 mm) remains, and use the round-nose pliers to create a small loop tight against the bugle bead.

TRY THiS:

Centipedes have at least 15 pairs of legs, but this beaded version can be made longer and leggier by increasing wire length, wire pieces for legs, and beads for the body and legs. Find pictures of centipedes to experiment with different species to make a collection of centipedes that vary in size

silverfish
drain dodger

Silverfish crop up in wet environments like bath drains and basements, but this less-than-slithery specimen just sits among its other exoskeletal friends, the centipede and earwig.

MATERIALS

SUPPLIES

» One 5" (13 cm) piece of 26-gauge peach- or white-coated wire

» Five 2" (5 cm) pieces of 26-gauge peach- or white-coated wire

» One 3" (7.6 cm) piece of 26-gauge peach- or white-coated wire

» One 8- x 12-mm black shell or silver teardrop bead

» Two 6-mm silver oval-tube spacer beads

» One 2- or 3-mm round silver spacer bead

» Two black or gray/silver seed beads

» E-6000 craft adhesive

TOOLS

» Wire cutters

» Round-nose pliers

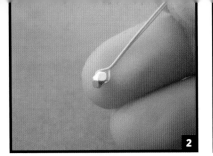

1. Cut the pieces of wire needed for this project. The 5" (13 cm) piece of wire is for the body of the silverfish; four of the five 2" (5 cm) pieces of wire are for the two feelers and six legs; one of the five 2" (5 cm) pieces of wire is for two of the elongated tail-like projections; and the 3" (7.6 cm) piece of wire is for the longest tail-like projection.

Thorax & Abdomen

2. Fold the 5" (13 cm) piece of 26-gauge wire in half, and thread the 2- or 3-mm round silver spacer bead onto the center of the wire. Pinch the wire closed around the bead.

3. Thread beads onto both pieces of wire in this order: 6-mm oval-tube spacer, 8- x 12-mm black shell teardrop. Spread the wires apart.

4. Thread the second 6-mm oval-tube spacer bead onto one of the wires, and loop the other wire through the opposite end of the spacer bead. Pull both ends tightly until the spacer bead is centered over the 8- x 12-mm black shell teardrop bead. Pull on the wires to secure the spacer bead tightly in place.

TRY THiS:

Look for matte silver beads that graduate from wide to narrow and have a segmented look to create a silverfish that is even more realistic.

Antennae & Feelers

5. Thread one seed bead onto each wire, one at a time. Loop the excess wire through the space between the two wires under the 6-mm oval-tube spacer bead, and pull the wire straight up for the antenna. Repeat on other side. Use flat-nose pliers as needed to create a tight loop so that the seed bead is firmly in place. Trim the excess antennae wire so that each antenna is approximately ½" (1 cm) long.

6. Wrap two of the 2" (5 cm) pieces of wire around the space between the horizontal 6-mm oval-tube spacer bead and the 8- x 12-mm black shell teardrop bead starting at the top of the silverfish body,

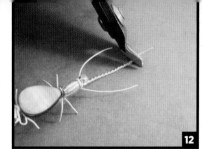

crisscross the wires underneath the body, and bring the wires back up to the top of the body so that they stick straight out to either side. Spread out the wires.

7. Use the wire cutters to trim the top wire on each side so that ¼" (6 mm) remains, and use the round-nose pliers to create an open loop to resemble the silverfish's feelers.

Legs & Filaments

8. Continue wrapping two of the 2" (5 cm) pieces of wire around the space between the 8- x 12-mm black shell teardrop bead and the vertical 6-mm oval-tube spacer bead following the instructions described in Step 6.

9. Use the wire cutters to trim the excess wire from each leg so that each leg is approximately ½" (1 cm) long. Use your fingers to create a slight bend in each leg.

10. Continue wrapping the last 2" (5 cm) piece of wire and the 3" (7.5 cm) piece of wire around the space between the vertical 6-mm oval-tube spacer bead and the 2- or 3-mm round silver spacer bead following the instructions described in Step 6.

11. Bring the two longest pieces of wire (from the 3" [7.6 cm] piece of wire) together underneath the silverfish's body and begin twisting them together tightly from the silverfish's body to the ends of the wire.

12. Use the wire cutters to trim the excess wire from the elongated tail-like projections (filaments) so that the center tail piece is ¾" (2 cm) long and the outside tail pieces are ½" (1.5 cm) long.

Finishing Touch

13. Place small dots of E-6000 craft adhesive on the underside of the silverfish where all of the wires are twisted between sets of beads to keep those wires from swiveling.

earwig
creeper

A fitting companion for the centipede and silverfish, the earwig moves about in damp, dark places with intimidating but harmless pincers.

MATERIALS

SUPPLIES
» One 4" (10 cm) piece of 28-gauge red- or black-coated wire
» Three 2" (5 cm) pieces of 28-gauge orange- or yellow-coated wire
» One 13-mm brown tube bead
» One 5-mm brown tube bead
» One black E bead
» One 4-mm round brown bead
» One 3.4-mm black drop bead

» Two lobster clasps
» E-6000 craft adhesive

(Note: Amber and tiger eye work well for the brown tube beads; copper or blackened bronze are best for the lobster clasp.)

TOOLS
» Wire cutters
» Round-nose pliers
» Flat-nose pliers

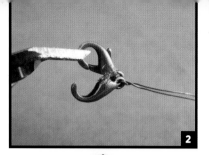

2

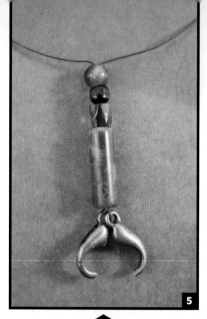

4

5

1. Cut the pieces of wire needed for this project. The 4" (10 cm) piece of wire is for the body of the earwig, and the three 2" (5 cm) pieces of wire are for the six legs.

Pincers
. . . .

2. Fold the 4" (10 cm) piece of 28-gauge wire in half. Thread both lobster clasps onto the center of the wire so that the inside of each lobster clasp hook faces the other, and pinch the wires closed.

3. Use the wire cutters to trim off part of the hook on each lobster clasp as shown in the picture. Remove as much of the movable clasp as possible from the outside and inside of the lobster clasp. If enough is removed, a spring will pop out, and flat-nose pliers can be used to completely remove the spring.

4. Lay flat the wire and lobster clasps, and adjust the lobster clasps so that they evenly touch one another. Apply a small amount of E-6000 craft adhesive to the seam where the lobster clasps touch one another. Allow to dry. This will keep the pincers from dangling and moving around.

Body
. . . .

5. Thread the following beads onto both wires in the following order: 13-mm brown tube bead, 5-mm brown tube bead, black E bead, 4-mm round brown bead. Spread apart the remaining wires.

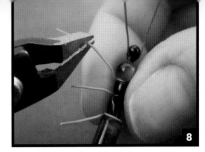

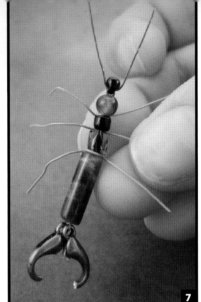

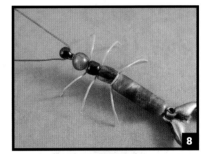

Antennae

6. Thread the 3.4-mm black drop bead onto one of the wires. Thread the other wire through the hole in the 3.4-mm black drop bead coming from the other direction. Pull both wires securely so that the drop bead fits snugly against the 4-mm round brown bead. Use flat-nose pliers as needed to pull the wires more tightly. Adjust the antennae so that they point straight up from the head of the earwig, and trim any excess wire so that the antennae are even and approximately ¾" (2 cm) long.

Legs

7. Wrap each of the three 2" (5 cm) pieces of 28-gauge wire around and between each of the three sets of beads below the 4-mm round brown bead starting from the top of the earwig's body, crisscrossing the wire underneath the body, and bringing the wire back up toward the top of the body so that the wires point straight out.

8. Use your fingers to curve the legs slightly before using the wire cutters to trim the excess leg wire so that the legs are approximately ⅜" (9 mm) long.

TRY THiS:

Cut thorns from a thorn bush to use for the earwig pincers. Drill small holes through the widest end of the thorns and glue them together side by side to keep them from dangling. Secure them to the earwig's body.

Resources

About the Author

Amy Kopperude grew up in Minnesota and was influenced by a painting grandma, a quilting mom and brother, a guitar-playing dad, and other talented people who supported her creative growth. She is an avid crafter who likes to dabble in all kinds of media and enjoys working with small, intricate pieces. She has an Etsy shop and a blog for sharing creations and ideas. Amy made 365 beaded spiders as part of a creativity project before exploring other beaded critters.